The original text, *What Every Chief Exec. ....   ииоuld Know...*was released in March 2007 and won the 2008 Police-Writers book of the year award (www.police-writers.com). The book was well received by the intended audience and many asked to see the conceptual models in a useable framework. That sparked the interest to write this application guide. Much of the advice came from police planners, mid-level and upper-level managers, both sworn and civilian from a wide variety of police agencies. These people routinely discuss agency performance with the chief executive and are best suited to influence performance measurement. Police agencies in the United States and Canada have adopted the concepts in the original text and this companion guide represents an extension of those concepts.

I am grateful to following practitioners for their advice and candor about this guide: Police Director Michael C. Walker, City of Paterson (New Jersey) and Adjunct Professor, Passaic County Community College; Major Christopher J. Andreychak, New Jersey State Police and Rutgers School of Criminal Justice; Cesar Lozado, Planning and Research Specialist, Charlotte County (Florida) Sheriff's Office; Lieutenant Terry Sterling, Pinellas County (Florida) Sheriff's Office; Corporal Julio Schrodel, Cape Coral (Florida) Police Department.

Jon M. Shane Associates is a law enforcement management firm specializing in research, evaluation and professional police services that improve organizational efficiency, validate business practices, identify deficiencies, and justify budgets with an eye toward performance. By analyzing policies, business processes and practices, we help law enforcement agencies make better operational decisions so they may consistently perform at their best.

As a partner with the agency, we confront the most challenging issues facing contemporary law enforcement, including:

- Analyzing claims of differential treatment
- Identifying better ways to spend law enforcement dollars
- Evaluating policies, programs and practices for effectiveness
- Developing an agency-wide business plan to define what it means to be effective and efficient

Visit **www.jonmshaneassociates.com** for more details.

Purpose	Relevant Chapters in the Primary Text
To define police performance and identify a logical structure for managing it	2
To understand performance in the context of the social and political purpose of the police	1
To embrace performance measurement as an integral part of police management	2
To understand the tangible nature of police performance measures	2
To translate policy implications into measurable business principles	1
To recognize the value of quantitative data in expressing "good performance"	3-4
To understand the techniques available for driving performance management	5-7

Implementation Strategy

Planning	Execution	Monitoring
Document What you Intend to Do...	*Do it...*	*Document What you Did*
• Mission • Desired Outcomes • Set Performance Standards	• Identify and Collect Performance Indicators • Link Performance to Budget • Affix Accountability	• Report Performance

"...chart a course for every endeavor that we take the people's money for, see how well we are progressing, tell the public how we are doing, stop the things that don't work, and never stop improving the things that we think are worth investing in."

— President William J. Clinton, on signing the
Government Performance and Results Act of 1993
August 3, 1993

This application guide should be used with *What Every Chief Executive Should Know: Using Data to Measure Police Performance,* and assumes familiarity with that text. This guide forges ahead by exploring six drivers of performance management that government and business can use to manage results. The intent is to synthesize the broad concepts of performance measurement discussed in the primary text with a comprehensible and useful management framework in this guide. The framework presented here takes a different approach than traditional police management is accustomed to working with. Traditional police management and supervision place an emphasis on compliance through command and control doctrine, and not on outcomes. From the top of the organization to the bottom, compliance is the watchword: Compliance with policy, rules, regulations, and verbal or written directives is at the root of police officers' activities, often at the expense of productivity and desired end outcomes. In this paradigm, unquestioned obedience to those orders, directives and policies govern how police work is delivered, leaving little room for initiative and independent thought. The slightest deviation from policy, even for the right reason, may result in negative discipline. [1] While compliance is somewhat necessary to control police activities based on the frequency and criticality of the activity (e.g., risk to someone's life), it should not triumph over outcomes in routine daily police operations (Alpert and Smith, 1994; LeBrec, 1982). Police departments exist to fulfill social and political needs. Meeting those needs is a labor-intensive, expensive endeavor subject to compromises, discretion and judgment. To determine whether those needs have been met, it is imperative for police departments to focus on the expected outcomes. This requires empowering police officers to solve recurring problems through creativity and initiative so the agency's intended benefits can be realized.

To push policing forward and to help organize what we know and what we could know about performance measurement, this guide borrows from various disciplines including policing, criminal justice, public administration and business management. The component parts of the model illustrated in this guide fit together to form a conceptual framework that police administrators can follow as they build a management structure that will produce measurable improvements, regardless of agency size. [2] The framework described in this

1

guide is not an abstract academic exercise. It should be embraced as a dynamic and logical approach to assessing and monitoring police performance to determine what worked, what did not, and why. This guide outlines the sequential steps necessary to develop a performance management model, which will help police executives attribute outcomes to the various programs and initiatives delivered by the police department, while concurrently recognizing the contribution individual employees make to the desired outcomes.

DEFINING POLICE PERFORMANCE

What is *police performance?* What does it look like? How would a police executive know if it existed? Indeed, defining it has been a conundrum for scholars and practitioners alike. Quite simply it should be defined as: _Police activity that results in quantifiable end outcomes_. Chief executives should understand how these eight words relate and interact. By disassembling and reversing the order of the definition, the capabilities and limitations of the definition become clear. When all is said and done, there should be no question about what the police are trying to achieve, what they actually achieved and what contributed to the intended outcome.

What is the Object? *End Outcomes.* An end outcome is an envisioned or desired state that results from operationally defined goals and objectives, culminating in measured performance. They are the results, impacts, consequences or intended effects of programs and services delivered by the agency. End outcomes must be thought of as the things the police department is trying to achieve, consistent with its stated mission (e.g., controlling fear, crime and disorder; reverence for law and authority; delivering public value through budgeting accountability).

Does the Object Exist? *Quantifiable.* In order to measure what the agency has been working toward (The end outcomes), it is necessary to reduce observations to numeric terms. This means defining performance measurement statements so outcomes can be counted, ordered and subjected to mathematical operations to determine if they are actually achieved. Measurement relies on counting occurrences and comparing changes in those occurrences to determine if they went up, down or stayed the same. When end outcomes are quantified, they become tangible. Their abstract existence translates into a definite and discernible form that indicates the outcome is likely to exist.

What is the Source of the Object? *Police Activity.* Police activities are the actions, the named processes, functions, or tasks that occur over time and have recognizable results (Output). They include all of the things the police do that contribute to a specified outcome (e.g., effecting arrests; following up with crime victims; following-up with offenders; [3] attending community meetings; processing prisoners; conducting directed patrols; effecting car stops; issuing traffic summonses; managing overtime; securing grant funds; answering requests for service). Police activities can be classified according to one of four attributes that represent an exhaustive list of the things the police do: Time, quantity, quality or cost. Most police departments routinely capture these data, which can be easily expressed in numeric terms for measurement against a predefined standard.

POLICE ACTIVITIES AS A BUSINESS PROCESS

Davenport (1993:5) defines business process as "A structured, measured set of activities designed to produce a specific output for a particular customer or market." This implies that police activities are the cornerstone of performance management because end outcomes *unequivocally depend* on how much and how well (e.g., the amount of public value and satisfaction generated) police officers perform the activities and functions assigned to them. Police activities typically combine to form a reliable pattern of work designed to produce a specific service toward a measurable end. Aggressive legislation, unfunded mandates, special interest groups and increased demand for public accountability are forcing police organizations to focus on their business process to ensure they comply with stringent regulations, enhance efficiency and deliver quality within their operations. Coordinating, managing and directing the various divisions of the police agency, the services they provide and how those services are delivered, is the agency's business process.

Police activities are the parts of the business process that do not include decision-making, insofar as strategy is concerned; decision-making occurs within policy constraints at the administrative, command and supervisory levels (Strategy) and the results of those decisions are executed at the operational level (Activities) (Figure 1. Also, see Table 6 for a rubric of accountability based on organizational function). How well a police agency performs is a matter of analyzing business processes to answer why things are carried out a certain way, to identify policy limitations and to map workflow to the activity level. There are three recognized business processes in police agencies: Management, support and operational.

Management Processes. Management processes govern the overall operation of the agency. Typical management processes include "executive governance" and "strategic management." Executive governance [4] includes customs, policies, laws and institutions affecting how the police department is directed, administered and controlled. It includes various internal and external relationships, bound by activities such as developing policy, budgeting, reviewing and complying with legal mandates, interacting with the media, maintaining labor relations and cooperating with community and political groups that help the agency achieve its desired outcomes. The principal relationships include the community at large (The citizenry), police management, elected officials and civic leaders. Other relationships include employees and unions, constituent groups, other facets of the criminal justice system, and regulators (State attorney general's office; police officer standards and training commission—POST; county district attorney/prosecutor's office; police unions). Executive governance is carried out at the administrative level (Chief/deputy chief), where the general direction of the department is established (Chapter 2).

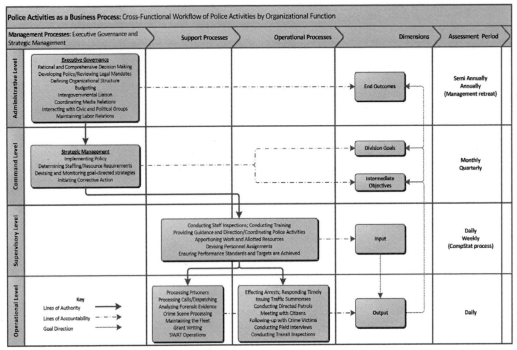

Figure 1

Strategic management is the managerial process of creating a vision for the organization, identifying division-level goals, setting priorities, developing and executing strategy developed by top administrators, and executing the strategy. Strategic management is usually carried out at the command level (Captain/ Lieutenant), where mid-level managers are responsible for division goals and intermediate objectives, bound by activities such as implementing policy, determining staffing and resource requirements, initiating corrective action, and devising goal-directed strategies, as necessary.

Support Processes. Support processes are ancillary functions that help sustain the agency's core purpose. They exist only to support managerial and operational processes, at one time or another all operational and management functions will make use of one or more support processes. Typical support processes include communications, prisoner detention, property/evidence storage, and records/identification among the many. The activities vary by function, however they usually include initiating actions to ensure performance standards, targets and goals (Division and organizational) are achieved.

Operational Processes. Operational processes create the primary value stream [5] and are part of the agency's core purpose (The mission). Operational processes include patrol, investigations (Personal crimes, property crimes, juveniles, and vice crimes) and traffic enforcement, which are designed to deliver a wide array of services to meet specified end outcomes. Operational activities include answering calls for service, following-up with crime victims, following-up with offenders, effecting arrests, issuing traffic summonses and conducting directed patrols among the many.

The agency's supervisory level (Sergeant/first-line supervisors) is responsible for operational and support processes, where they exercise operational control over the workforce including production of outputs and processes that help sustain individual productivity. The line employees (Police officers, detectives and civilian staff) report to supervisors and are responsible for executing activities, either directed by a supervisor or self-initiated, that eventually lead to the organization's goals.

The definition of police performance used in this guide is deceptively simple and it is easy to understand how the activities of each level of the organization combine to form a process that leads to the desired goals. The definition is easily operationalized and should be easily understood by those who have contact with it, yet it is also limited. It is limited because it cannot account for the intangible qualities of "personality" that are essential for good police work, such as judgment and leadership. Competent supervisors and command-rank personnel must observe, reinforce and evaluate these characteristics to ensure police personnel treat their customers with fairness, dignity and competence.

THE IMPORTANCE OF MEASUREMENT

Measuring the *"things the police do"* has implications for both personnel and the organization. In particular, focusing on outcomes instead of compliance supports participatory management, which promotes democratic ideals that are crucial for a healthy police organization and for community relations (Pace, 1989; Pateman, 1975; Rhoades, 1991). Thus, performance management supports employee participation, organizational democracy and community relations and manifests itself in the following ways:

- **"Better decision-making:** Provides managers with information to perform their management control functions;
- **Performance appraisal:** Links both individual and organizational performance to aspects of personnel management and motivates employees;
- **Accountability:** Fosters responsibility on the part of managers;
- **Service delivery:** It improves public service performance through productivity, effectiveness, quality and timeliness;

- **Public participation:** Clear reporting of performance measures can stimulate the public to take a greater interest in and provide more encouragement for government employees to provide quality services;
- **Improvement of civic discourse:** Helps to make public deliberations about service delivery more factual and specific;" [6]
- **Organizational citizenship (OCB):** "Job-related behaviors which are discretionary, not formally recognized by the organizational reward system, and in the aggregate, promote the effective functioning of the organization" (Moorman, Neihoff, and Organ, 1993:209). [7]

Above all, it is *good management* because the ethical obligations of public-sector managers are weighty. Police resources are collectively owned, paid for with the citizens' money. This means the police are accountable to the taxpayers for where resources are committed; how much resources are invested in particular programs; and the outcomes of those programs. The performance management framework described in this guide comports nicely with a rubric under which police agencies can operate to ensure they fulfill several public managerial responsibilities:

1) Public Oversight
   a) Department mission
   b) Accountability
   c) Program and policy evaluation
2) Performance Attributes
   a) Responsiveness
   b) Equity
   c) Effectiveness
   d) Efficiency
   e) Due process
3) Social Values
   a) Crime and fear control
   b) Reverence for law and authority
   c) Customer service
   d) Public confidence
4) Agency Management
   a) Productivity
   b) Resource allocation
   c) Staff morale
   d) Cost control

AN INSTITUTIONAL COMMITMENT TO PERFORMANCE

Author Mark Friedman (2005:87) commented that people fear having their performance measured primarily because at one time or another, it was used to punish them. While this is clearly a major source of employee resistance echoed by other experts, researchers also identify several other issues that challenge implementation and organizational commitment:

Paul Arveson (1998) [8]	Howard Rohm (2002) [9]
The costs outweigh the benefits. What will we find that we didn't already know?	Fear of measurement and new systems
Some tasks will be labor intensive: Metrics definition, software development, data collection	Lack of common definitions and terms
We have only limited control over results. Why should we be held accountable for things we can't control?	Inconsistent or weak buy-in, and lack of understanding
The results will be used against us	Visions and strategies that are poorly defined and understood, not actionable, and not linked to individual actions
Management will misuse or misinterpret the results. The process will be gamed	Treating budgeting as separate from strategy development
They will score us by inappropriate or unfair standards	Measures that are set independently of the performance framework, or measures with no ownership
Too much complexity: There are numerous systems and assessment criteria; how will we combine them all?	No performance targets, or targets that are set too high or too low
It's too big and ambitious and expensive to deploy a performance measurement system in this entire organization. We can't afford such large-scale efforts	Little or no strategic feedback
	Lack of meaningful employee involvement

The framework proposed in this guide can overcome most if not all of these objections because it is employee-centric and value-driven with an emphasis on outcomes, not necessarily on formal agency rules and compliance (Cordner, 1989). This framework resembles *"The Corporate Strategy"* method advocated by Kenneth R. Andrews (1980), which emphasizes setting goals, designing the organizational structure and allocating resources to achieve the desired ends. The bedrock of a police agency is its personnel. Personnel produce the value stream for the agency, that is, the tasks they are assigned are the *products* offered by the agency. The better the product, the better the agency. Consequently, organizational effectiveness rests directly on personnel productivity. Improving productivity comes from establishing a commitment to and investment in personnel. This investment is a long-term process that must involve all personnel who have an interest in improving the agency, particularly the managers and supervisors (Whitaker et al., 1982). To do this, the chief executive must serve as the sponsor and internal champion, binding himself or herself both intellectually and emotionally to a stated course of action. Sponsorship provides legitimacy to the process, while championship provides the energy and dedication to follow through.

Performance management does not just happen—the agency's leaders serve as process champions and gradually, employees who feel affiliated and are involved in decisions that affect them, will believe the agency is sincere and will embrace its methods and goals. In a performance management model, the most important quality for the chief executive and his or her subordinate managers to display is "interpersonal competence," which fosters "a spirit of cooperation in problem solving and embracing, creating, and implementing change" (Delorenzi, Shane and Amendola, 2006:1).

Every police organization should strive to provide high quality services at a reasonable cost, but achieving desired outcomes is not possible without a high-performing workforce. Contemporary police leaders realize that their success, however "success" may be defined, depends on the workforce. Chief executives and command staff officers recognize employees are their most valuable asset whose potential can and should be maximized. Top administrators understand the importance of aligning people with current and future organizational goals, but they often lack a framework for managing the entire process. The potential solutions rest in the framework presented in this guide. Once top administrators develop a suitable model for their agency, they can better assess the skills and competencies of the workforce to help meet program and agency outcomes. If a gap exists between the current workforce and the ideal workforce, then top administrators should analyze that gap and tailor adjustments as necessary.

After the agency conducts a "gap analysis," it can direct employees into specific training programs that develop knowledge, skills and abilities (KSA's) to meet the agency's current and anticipated future demands, thus developing future leaders (Day, 2001). As employees are trained, their interests and performance should be matched with the agency's needs, in a framework of continuous performance assessment as it relates to the agency's desired outcomes; it is imperative the agency constantly ensure performance and training goals are aligned with the agency's mission. Why train all detectives to investigate organized crime when the agency does not investigate organized crime?—the agency refers organized crime investigations to the state police or the FBI. Unfortunately, KSA development is often the first budget item to be cut, because there is often a disjunction between the training employees receive (Input) and the demonstrated performance (Output and outcome). Because KSA development is a recurring and endless expense, there is a tremendous need to measure the return on the investment (ROI). In this sense, the performance management framework descried in this guide connects the total cost of training and KSA development to the increase (Or decrease) in employee effectiveness. The framework enables the organization to collect pre- and post-training metrics that can be calibrated against a variety of standards that empirically demonstrates the value of various training initiatives. Decisions based on these measurements are more rational and credible because the effort is quantifiable.

DEFINING PERFORMANCE MANAGEMENT

Performance management is a systematic effort to improve performance through an ongoing process of establishing desired outcomes, setting performance standards, then collecting, analyzing and reporting on streams of data to improve individual and collective performance. There is a distinction between performance measurement and performance management. Performance measurement compares observed (Actual) levels of performance to pre-established targets. To be effective, performance measurement must align with the organization's mission. Performance management is the process of using performance measurement data to manage and improve individual and collective performance by identifying what has been achieved. Performance measurement is an essential component of performance management, not the other way around (Artley, Ellison and Kennedy, 2001:4; Bourne, Franco and Wilkes, 2003:15).

To represent how performance management works, a cause and effect diagram (Figure 2) is used to reveal the important relationships among component parts and to provide additional insight into process behavior. A cause and effect diagram explores the *causes* (Six drivers of performance management) that result in a single *effect* (Performance management); it graphically illustrates the relationship between the given outcome and all the factors that influence that outcome. Arranged causes according to their level of importance results in a visual association and hierarchy of processes.

The cause and effect diagram compares the relative importance of different objectives, which supports the fundamental premise of performance management: *To orient the agency for success.* Success is often in the eye of the beholder; it means different things to different people, something police scholars and practitioners have debated for years. The most important question that arises when discussing the word "success" is: *Compared to what?* How does one know if the patrol division is successful? How does one know if the new domestic violence program is working? To determine whether strategies or programs "worked" is a matter of contrasting them against something else, namely a performance standard. As defined here, "success" means measures of time, quantity, quality or cost calibrated against a predefined standard, typically expressed as improvement over the baseline.

Time	Quantity	Quality	Cost
• Cycle time • Response time • Hours per unit	• Crime/victimization rate • Workload demands • Enforcement actions	• % of citizens satisfied • % effectiveness • Degree of courtesy	• Cost per unit • Overtime • % under budget

These four measurable data sources can be compared to virtually everything police departments do as a business. Police departments do a great deal of work every day, but they are pulled off course every day to put out "brush fires" that erupt. "Brush fire" management, also termed "management by crisis," distracts the agency from its core business, its mission. When distractions do come (Because they are inevitable in policing), a performance management

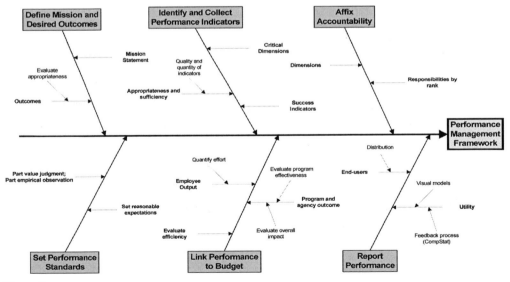

Figure 2

framework helps keep the agency on track to meet its goals. Dealing with crises is the business of the police. However, when the crisis is over, there must be a static model the chief executive can return to as he or she steers the ship. This is why it is imperative to have a written business plan documenting a course of action, which defines:

What the agency does *(Mission)* and what it plans to achieve within its stated mission *(Desired Outcomes)* → what it will compare performance against *(Performance Standards)* → what data will be collected to measure that performance *(Performance Indicators)* → what the costs are to achieve a particular level of performance *(Link Performance to the Budget)* → who is responsible for the performance *(Accountability)* and → what the results of performance are, what can be replicated and what must be done differently in the future *(Report Performance)*

Box 1

This model helps managers understand the strategic management process (Chapter 2) and how to keep the agency on track to become a high performing organization. This model also helps managers overcome vague impressions, conjecture and anecdotal evidence that programs are "working" and the agency is "successful" by using empirical data to support decisions.

TERMINOLOGY

To ensure managers understand all the processes in the performance management framework, terminology must be defined; lack of clear definitions is an oft-cited objection to performance management. These are the terms used throughout this guide specifically and performance management in general:

Table 1 Common Terminology used in Performance Management	
Accountability	An obligation or willingness to accept responsibility and to proffer a statement or explanation of reasons, causes, or motives to account for one's actions.
Baseline	Starting point for subsequent measurements as of a specific date; baseline data is used to provide a starting point for subsequent measurements and comparisons.
Critical Dimensions	The principle aspects of a goal that, if achieved, are intended to assure the goals are accomplished.
Effectiveness	The ability to achieve stated goals or objectives, judged in terms of both output and impact; the relationship of an organization's outputs to what an organization intended to accomplish. Effectiveness is expressed as a percentage and is calculated by: 1) the difference between the baseline data and the actual activity; divided by 2) the difference between the baseline data and the target data.

Efficiency	The degree to which output is achieved in terms of input (resources allocated) as expressed by ratio; the quality of being efficient. Efficiency is a measure of performance insofar as management may set objectives and plan schedules and for which staff members may be held accountable through minimizing waste, expense, or unnecessary effort. Efficiency is the reciprocal of productivity.
Input	The specific resources, including human and financial, that an organization must invest to produce the output necessary to achieve the desired end outcome.
Intermediate Objective	The process of defining and monitoring strategies and changes necessary to achieve the stated end outcome; assessing short-term progress toward the stated end outcome—interim progress.
Outcome	A measure of the degree to which a service has achieved its goal, and as defined, met the needs of its recipients in terms of quantity and quality.
Output	The direct products or services of personnel activities. Output typically measures the amount of something (e.g., the number of...; the percent of...; the ratio of...).
Performance Indicators	Qualitative or quantitative measurements that demonstrate meaningful steps are being taken to achieve a stated goal.
Performance Measurement Statement	A written declaration by the agency that conveys precisely what, where, when, how and how much the agency expects to achieve of something being measured.
Performance Standard	A measurable number specifying the minimum acceptable outcome for an organizational element or practice, typically expressed as degree of excellence or level of requirement that meets or exceeds predefined specifications. See target.
Productivity	As a measure of efficiency, expresses the ratio of output to input resources, usually per a defined metric. Productivity is the reciprocal of efficiency.
Quality	The degree to which a service meets the expectations or requirements, stated and un-stated, of the customer. Quality is expressed as a percentage of the number of units produced correctly/total number of units produced.
Success Indicator	A particular value or characteristic used to measure outcome or output.
Target	The part of a performance measure that establishes the desired level to be reached in a defined time period, usually stated as an improvement over the baseline.
Timeliness	The frequency with which services are provided within the time required and the established deadlines. Timeliness is expressed as a percentage of the number of units produced on time/total number of units produced.

▶ **Policy Implications**

The approach to performance management is to identify, capture and analyze a "large number and wide variety of performance indicators" that lead toward "better practice" (Behn, 2004:21). Measuring performance is intended to improve societal "good" (i.e., quality of life) while concurrently slowing the "bad" (i.e., wasteful spending; victimization and public disorder) (Metzenbaum, 2006:6). What does this mean for your agency? By applying the model presented here, top police administrators can align activities and core processes with four business principles that result in a corporate culture of accountability (Chapter 1). The four business principles and their processes are:

1) **Financial Accountability:** Government spends its money as authorized, with as little waste as possible, represented through:
    a) Budgeting
    b) Cost-benefit analysis
    c) Cost-effectiveness analysis

2) **Ethical Accountability:** Agencies operate honestly, without conflict of interest, self-dealing, other forms of fraud, or abuse of the power of governmental authority, represented through:
    a) Integrity
    b) Professionalism
    c) Equity

3) **Democratic Accountability:** Government agencies do what their citizens want and need, engaging citizens and their elected representatives in understanding trade-offs and making well-informed choices among competing priorities. Government agencies treat people civilly and courteously, unless there are strong justifications not to, so people do not resent or resist government because it has acted in a rude, slow, or inappropriate manner, represented through:
    a) Transparency and civility
    b) Image and reputation
    c) Partnership building

4) **Performance Accountability:** Government agencies and their employees work intelligently and diligently to deliver effective and cost-efficient government programs (Metzenbaum, 2006:6), represented through:
    a) Diligence and competence
    b) Efficiency and effectiveness
    c) Process and impact evaluation

▶ Six Drivers of Performance Management

DEFINE A MISSION AND DESIRED OUTCOMES

Mission Statement. There is some debate about the utility and relevance of mission statements in policing (Mastrofski, 1999); however, others agree they serve a valuable function for police agencies (Schroeder, Lombardo and Strollo, 1995; Weiss, 1996; Weiss and Piderit, 1999; Wilson, 1989). DeLone (2007:221) noted, "You cannot adequately evaluate police performance if you do not first examine what it is police say they are doing." To determine what the organization does, it is imperative to identify the mandates imposed on the department. Formal external mandates are typically found in state or federal laws, court decisions, city ordinances, regulatory guidelines (e.g., state attorney general's policies; POST policies) and city charters. Informal internal mandates are often embedded in "cultural norms or expectations" and accepted past practices of constituent groups and key stakeholders (Bryson, 1995:65). This is why it is imperative to analyze the organization's strengths, weaknesses, opportunities and threats (e.g., S.W.O.T analysis) [10] with key stakeholders, so the organization can clarify what it does and what it prioritizes. The mission statement should also provide a sense of identity for the organization (Denhardt, 2001:249) as well as define its core purpose (e.g., the reason for its existence). It is around this concept that the organization builds its performance management model.

The organization's mission often reflects the management style of the chief executive. [11] This means there may be an emphasis on service, on formal legalistic enforcement or on order maintenance (Wilson, 1968). Regardless of the management style adopted by the agency, before the mission statement is promulgated, there must be commitment from the rest of the organization to execute the stated purpose. When creating the mission statement, the chief executive should circulate a few drafts to ensure each layer of the organization has had an opportunity to review and comment about: 1) what the agency's core business is today; 2) who its customers are; and 3) what its business principles are. The mission statement shown in box 2 identifies those elements. It also comports well with the four business principles named earlier that can foster a culture of accountability:

Mission Statement

To _protect and serve_ the _public_ by delivering _legitimate_, _consistent_, _economical_ police services that result in the highest level of _public value and satisfaction_

Box 2

1) **The agency's core business today:** _Protection and service_ → To safeguard the rights of all people within its jurisdiction to be free from criminal intrusion in their persons, houses and possessions, and to live in peace. Protection and service are built through a wide array of law enforcement services, including crime prevention techniques, reactive and proactive investigations and problem-solving partnerships directed toward community cohesion. Protection and service are the basic social and political needs the organization intends to achieve.

2) **Who its customers are:** _The public_ → The "public" are the citizens within the agency's jurisdiction; they are all those who summon or have contact with the police whether for mere inquiry, as a victim, witness, complainant or offender.

3) **What its business principles are:** _Legitimacy, consistency, economy, public value and satisfaction_ → Business principles establish the agency's management philosophy, core values, functional objectives and resource objectives. There are four business principles embedded in the agency's mission, each with a degree of accountability attached:

   a) **Legitimate:** _Ethical accountability_ → built through constant integrity, professionalism and equity;

   b) **Consistent:** _Democratic accountability_ → built through constant transparency and civility, reliability, image, reputation and partnership building;

   c) **Economical:** _Fiscal accountability_ → built through constant budgeting, cost-benefit analysis, and cost-effectiveness analysis;

   d) **Public Value and Satisfaction:** _Performance accountability_ → built through constant diligence and competence, efficiency, effectiveness, productivity and quality.

The mission statement is essential because it forms the basis upon which the organization builds its policies, programs and ultimately delivers its services. The moment people in the agency, especially the chief executive, begin to lose sight of the mission, there is a tendency to stray off course from the organization's basic social and political purpose. When this occurs, resources are wasted; this tends to lead to inefficiency and ineffectiveness.

Desired Outcomes. [12] From the mission, it is necessary to operationalize concrete goals. Operationalization is the process of defining the activities (The operations) that will measure the mission, through quantifiable observations. The process begins by defining appropriate outcomes. Since police resources are scarce and finite, they must be apportioned according to priority. This means, police administrators should avoid pursuing programs that do not align with the mission or have been shown not to achieve their intended outcomes, or pursuing unrealistic or lofty goals they cannot achieve. [13] Too often, goals are set but they are not connected to the agency's mission. This is especially true of sub-units in the organizational structure, where the sub-unit becomes more self-serving than actually supporting the agency's overall mission (O'Hara, 2005). The goals of the sub-unit must connect to the agency's mission. While it may be difficult to break with tradition or with community sentiment, the resources can probably be used better elsewhere. [14] This model defines four outcome measures:

Desired Outcomes
1. Controlling fear and crime
2. Delivering public value through budgeting accountability
3. Reverence for law and authority
4. Satisfying customers through service and accountability

Box 3

These four outcomes are multidimensional and reflect the elements of the mission statement (Chapter 2). A multidimensional model means there is no single best way to express performance; rather, multiple dimensions better express what the agency does because they include things beyond just controlling crime, such as service delivery, financials and legitimacy. These outcomes also represent an exhaustive list of the things police do, meaning everything they do can be categorized under one of the four outcomes. Once the outcomes are identified, the next step is to set performance standards.

SET PERFORMANCE STANDARDS

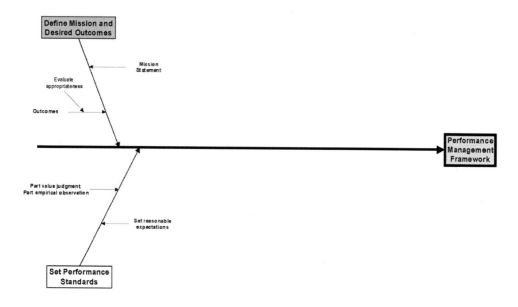

A law enforcement agency has an obligation to the community it serves as well as its employees. For the community, the agency must declare what level of service they expect to deliver. For the employees, the organization must declare what it expects from them in terms of performance. In this respect, performance standards are one of the most important aspects of performance management because they specify the minimum acceptable outcome for the agency's goals. Jones (1998:110) commented, "Operating without performance standards can doom a department and its officers to work in an energy-draining atmosphere full of inconsistency, bickering and chaos. Operating with performance standards enables supervisors to bring sanity, fairness and consistency to supervisory tasks, enhance performance levels, and makes promotions, awards and disciplinary actions fair." In terms of equitable promotion decisions, in July 2007, the United States Court of Appeals for the 5th Circuit ruled against the state of Texas (Defendant) for failing to account for how it reached the decision to deny an employee a request for a transfer. In *Alvarado, v. Texas Rangers, Department of Public Safety*, [15] the plaintiff argued she was denied a transfer to a preferred assignment because of her sex; the defendant (Texas Rangers) argued she was denied the transfer because she received lower performance scores. The Court held, in pertinent part:

1. "An employer's denial of a transfer may be the objective equivalent of the denial of a promotion, and thus qualify as an 'adverse employment action' for purposes of Title VII, even if the new position would not have entailed an increase in pay or other tangible benefits, [and];

2. ...[the] employer failed to articulate a *clear and reasonably specific* basis for its *subjective assessment* of trooper's interview *performance*, as required to satisfy its burden of producing evidence tending to show that it had a legitimate, non-discriminatory reason for not appointing her to the Rangers, (Emphasis mine) [and];

3. ...DPS offered neither an explanation nor evidence of how or why the interviewers arrived at those scores, DPS provided no evidence of why the board rated the other candidates, particularly the ten men who were selected for the Rangers, higher than trooper, and so the score, standing alone, was at least as consistent with discriminatory intent as it was with nondiscriminatory intent because trooper may well have received the relatively low interview score on account of her sex."

Perhaps this decision is not "ground breaking." However, it does highlight the need for the agency to self-impose limits on its discretion, articulate, in writing, an objective basis for assignment/transfer decisions, and communicate what it expects from its employees (i.e., performance standards) (Chapter 2). A written performance framework helps the agency define the logic behind and justification for decisions about what it is they are trying to achieve and the acceptable level of performance. Otherwise, bias or favoritism influence employment decisions; supervisors and managers are not working toward a particular outcome; and the workforce does not have a definable purpose. Performance standards not only help correct these issues but they are essential for measuring effort and outcome.

With Performance Standards
1. Unanimity of purpose
2. Fairness (supervision, promotions, assignments, awards and disciplinary action)
3. Consistency
4. Delimits individual productivity

Without Performance Standards
1. Lack of clear purpose
2. Temperamental environment
3. Inconsistency (supervision, promotions, awards and disciplinary action)
4. Independent action toward no articulated end

Box 4

Over the last forty years, researchers have discovered at least three ways performance standards engender positive action in employees:

- Creating reasonable performance standards may give employees "a better sense of what is expected of them...The objectives are much clearer and less ambiguous" (Wilson, 1968:53);
- The employee "always tried to perform according to his most concrete and specific understanding of the control system" (Skolnick, 1968:180); and
- "...the essential elements for any control system include the development of standards for performance, observations for deviations from these standards, determination of the causes of deviation and implementation of corrective action" (Kuykendall, 1975 in Meagher, 1986:69).

Kuykendall's observations meet contemporary standards of police administration, business management and public administration as they relate to developing a performance management system.

Performance standards and targets are the numeric values of a performance metric that must be achieved by a given date; targets must specify the metric and be time-bound. Forecasting techniques (Chapter 6) can help police executives, managers and supervisors predict future targets for a variety of best and worst case scenarios and are ideal for planning purposes. For each desired outcome in this model (*Controlling Fear and Crime; Delivering Public Value through Budgeting Accountability; Reverence for Law and Authority; Satisfying Customers through Service and Accountability*) the chief executive, together with the command staff, must specify the minimum acceptable outcome for that dimension. Performance standards are typically expressed as a degree of excellence or some level of requirement that meets or exceeds predefined specifications. For example, the desired outcome Controlling Fear and Crime might have as its performance standard a crime rate of 6,404 per 100,000 (Numeric value) for the next calendar year (Time-bound); for the outcome *Delivering Public Value through Budgeting Accountability*, the performance standard might be increasing budget compliance to 96% for the next fiscal year; for the outcome *Satisfying Customers Through Service and Accountability*, the performance standard might be a citizen satisfaction rating of 90% within the next two years.

Performance Standards			
Outcome	Nexus to the Mission Statement	Numeric Value	Time Limit
Reduce crime rate	→ Protection	→ 6,404 per 100,000	→ December 31, 2008
Increase budget compliance	→ Economy	→ 96%	→ (FY) July 31, 2008
Reduce citizen complaints	→ Legitimacy	→ 25%	→ December 31, 2008
Increase citizen satisfaction rating	→ Service; Public value; citizen satisfaction	→ 90%	→ December 31, 2010

Box 5

The best approach is to identify a few specific goals for each sub-unit of the department under each desired outcome, then establish intermediate objectives for each division represented on the organizational chart that have measurable goals that lead toward the desired outcome. Establishing intermediate objectives includes defining and monitoring strategies and changes that are necessary to achieve the desired outcomes. They serve to assess short-term or interim progress toward the stated end outcome. For example, the patrol division and the criminal investigations division should each have goals that contribute to controlling fear and crime. Not every division of the department will contribute to each desired outcome, since some divisions are operational and some are administrative with altogether different functions. However, the collective effect of each division's outcomes means the agency as a *whole* is delivering on its stated mission.

This part of the development process is critical because if the workforce perceives the performance standards set by the agency as unreasonable, the outcomes will not be achieved. The workforce will stop striving to achieve the established standards because they will feel that nothing they do will help them meet the target. Worse yet, they may sabotage the work product because they feel the agency is pressuring them needlessly and unreasonably to satisfy some ulterior motive instead of the goal that is actually articulated. This often occurs when performance standards are set too high, given the current resources and employee skill set. The old adage *unreasonable expectations produce reasonable results* is a fallacy; the workforce will shut down in the face of seemingly insurmountable performance standards.

Setting performance standards is part value judgment and part empirical observation. A value judgment is a subjective decision or opinion, rendered by the chief executive with input from the command staff, about how high to set a particular standard. The "value" aspect is based on beliefs, typically derived from professional judgment, past practice or management theory about what someone believes the agency can realistically achieve. Empirical observations are based on statistics derived from various sources such as databases (e.g., computer-aided dispatch system; records management system), hard-copy documents (e.g., field interview reports; incident reports; traffic summonses; internal affairs records; budgets; investigation reports) or other sources that reveal the nature, magnitude or seriousness of conditions and actual past practice (Chapter 3). [16] The chief's decision about where to set performance standards is usually derived from a combination of empirical data, past agency experience and management philosophy (e.g., community policing or traditional).

Table 2 Data Sources for Performance Standards	
• Research findings	• Technically developed norms for similar programs
• Legal mandates	• Past agency trends/historical data
• Expert opinion	• Private sector results for similar programs
• Geographical areas within the same jurisdiction	• Industry/government/professional standards
• Similar jurisdictions	• Community expectations

From the empirical data, baseline measures can be established. Baseline data establishes the dataset as of a given date and provides a starting point for subsequent measurements and comparisons (e.g., crime rates; clearance rates; victimization rates; use of force rates; unit costs per activity; compliance rates; convictions rates). Baseline data is imperative since it is the standard against which individual, program or agency performance will be measured. Improvement over the baseline is typically considered "good" performance. [17]

Once performance standards are agreed upon, the next step is to identify and collect data that indicate the outcome is being achieved. These data are known as performance indicators.

IDENTIFY AND COLLECT PERFORMANCE INDICATORS

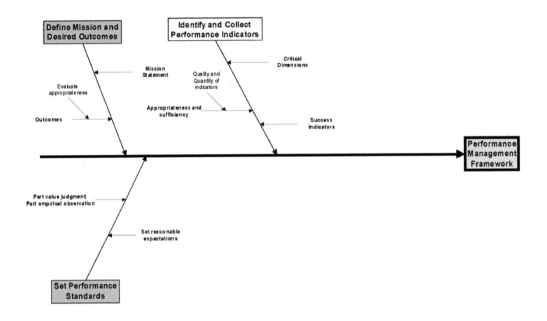

There is a great deal of value expressing performance in numeric terms, foremost is that measurement allows for improvement. Numbers offer readers a sense of comfort in their own knowledge, and reports supported by statistics are generally more persuasive and more credible (Chapter 4). Performance indicators are the route to measuring success and influencing policy. For each desired outcome, you must identify and collect numeric measures that demonstrate meaningful steps are being taken to achieve the stated outcome. All of these measures should be appropriate and sufficient. An appropriate measure is one that logically reflects the desired outcome. For example, when trying to control fear and crime, appropriate performance indicators include the number and disposition of arrests effected; percent of cases cleared by arrest; repeat offender rate; number of victim follow-up visits by detectives; percent of citizens that are "fearful" via community surveys (Figure 2). Sufficiency is the range of performance indicators used to measure a desired outcome. When trying to control fear and crime, it is important to capture several different indices that measure the construct, not just rely on a single measure; there will undoubtedly be a wide range of indicators that should be captured for each desired outcome (Chapter 2, *Adopting Suitable Performance Measures for Your Agency*).

Before performance indicators are collected, the structure of each performance dimension must be described and may take the form shown in figures 3-6; the components include: 1) the goal; 2) the critical dimensions; 3) the success indicators and 4) the performance indicators (Chapter 2). The *goal*, or outcome, is a measure of the degree to which a service has achieved its intended effect, and as defined, has met the needs of its recipients in terms of quantity and quality. Goals must be measurable to ensure the desired end state is achieved. The *critical dimensions* are the principle aspects of a goal that, if achieved, are intended to assure the goal is accomplished. Critical dimensions are typically derived from a theory or from empirical observation. For example, it is believed (and it is logical to assume) that to control fear and crime (a goal), a few different things must occur:

1) Crime and criminal victimization must be reduced;
2) Holding offenders accountable must be increased;
3) Fear and blight must be reduced;
4) Feelings of personal safety must be enhanced; and
5) The guarantee of safety while in public places must be enhanced (See figure 3).

Critical dimensions separate the activities the police engage in, to create conceptual order and to organize the performance indicators. This is the systematic nature of performance management because the activities the police engage in measure different things and they must be arranged in a logical order. Critical dimensions are measured through *success indicators*.

Success indicators define the attributes or characteristics to be measured; they are a particular value or characteristic used to measure outcome or output. The question we are asking is this: *If we are to reduce crime and criminal victimization, then where will we see success?* In this case, success will come from the crime and victimization rate, the number of index crimes (FBI Uniform Crime Report, Part I crimes) and the number of status offenses, to name just a few. Success is predicated on the activities of the police; the logic is the *"things the police do"* (i.e., their activities) should contribute to improving the "good" while slowing the "bad."

The next step is to identify *performance indicators*. Performance indicators are qualitative or quantitative measurements that demonstrate meaningful steps are being taken toward the stated goal. For example, workforce activities such as the number and disposition of arrests, the number of directed patrols and the percentage of cases cleared by arrest are the things the police officers do that contribute to the stated goal. The logical flow for controlling fear and crime appears in figure 3; [18] figures 4-6 are examples of three other performance dimensions, which satisfy the entire spectrum of desired outcomes as defined by the mission statement.

Once the agency identifies the performance dimensions, a series of performance measurement statements that describe what success will look like should be developed (Chapter 2). For example, under the outcome *Controlling Fear and Crime*, a performance measurement statement for the critical dimension *reducing crime and criminal victimizations*, might contain the following components and read like this:

Table 3 Performance Measurement Statement

Reduce **total index crimes citywide** from **2,300** in FY 2007 to **1,955 (-15%)** in **FY 2008** by **increasing enforcement action**

Table 4 Components of a Performance Measurement Statement

Basic measure: Total index crimes	**Success indicator**
Direction: Reduce	
Object: Index crimes (2,300)	**Baseline**
Value: 1,955 (-15%)	**Target**
Where: Citywide	
When: FY 2008	**Time-bound**
How: Increasing enforcement action	**Performance indicators**

Modified from SEARCH, 2003:10-13

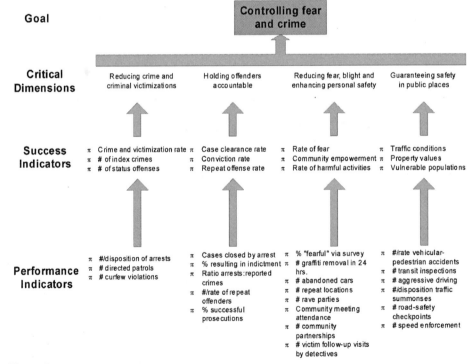

Figure 3

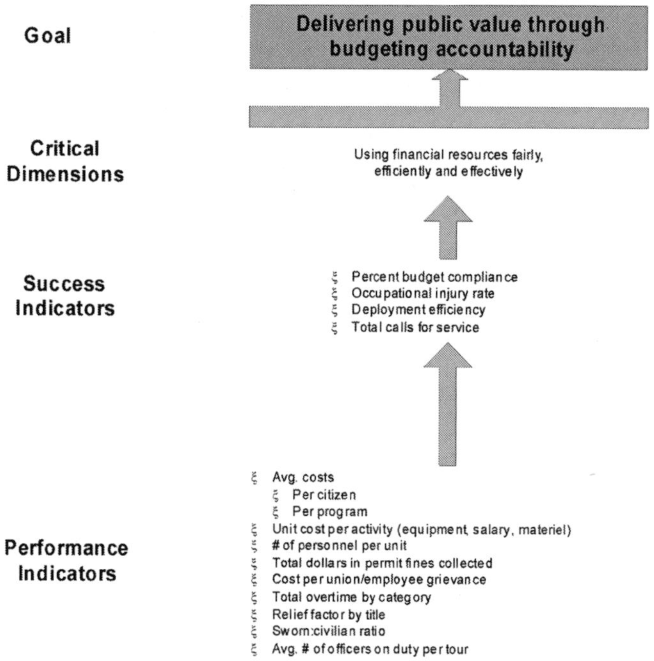

Goal

Delivering public value through budgeting accountability

Critical
Dimensions

Using financial resources fairly,
efficiently and effectively

Success
Indicators

- Percent budget compliance
- Occupational injury rate
- Deployment efficiency
- Total calls for service

Performance
Indicators

- Avg. costs
  - Per citizen
  - Per program
- Unit cost per activity (equipment, salary, materiel)
- # of personnel per unit
- Total dollars in permit fines collected
- Cost per union/employee grievance
- Total overtime by category
- Relief factor by title
- Sworn:civilian ratio
- Avg. # of officers on duty per tour

Figure 4

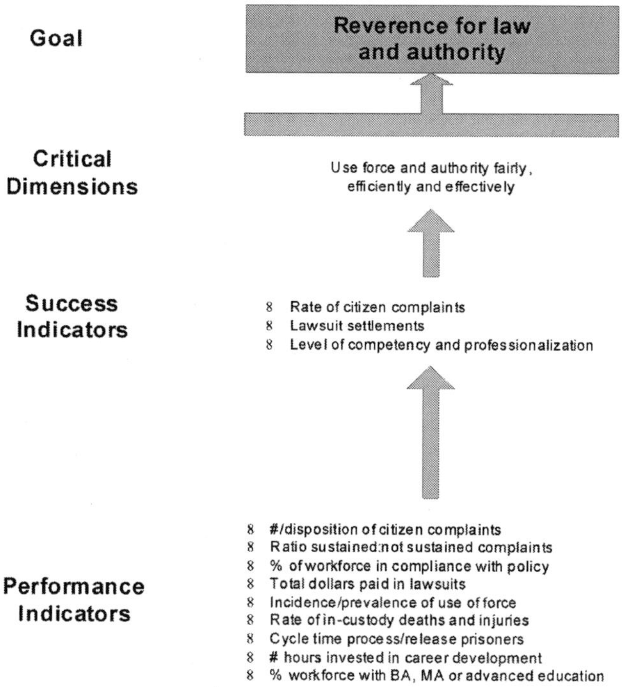

Goal

**Reverence for law
and authority**

Critical
Dimensions

Use force and authority fairly,
efficiently and effectively

Success
Indicators

- Rate of citizen complaints
- Lawsuit settlements
- Level of competency and professionalization

Performance
Indicators

- #/disposition of citizen complaints
- Ratio sustained:not sustained complaints
- % of workforce in compliance with policy
- Total dollars paid in lawsuits
- Incidence/prevalence of use of force
- Rate of in-custody deaths and injuries
- Cycle time process/release prisoners
- # hours invested in career development
- % workforce with BA, MA or advanced education

Figure 5

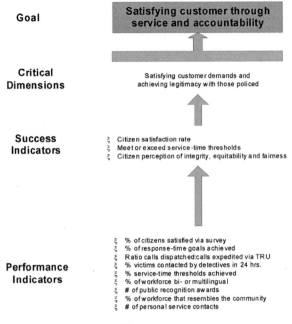

Figure 6

After the agency defines the data elements it will capture, the next step is to link performance to the budget to get a sense of what it will cost to meet those standards.

LINK PERFORMANCE TO THE BUDGET

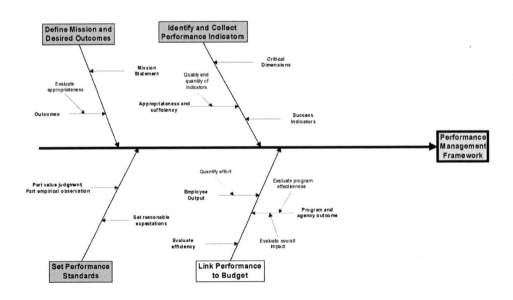

Policing is an expensive endeavor and, as such, demands those responsible for its administration account for the resources appropriated for its operation. This process begins by linking performance to the budget, so decisions can be made about where resources are expended and for what purpose. Linking the budget to performance shows how resources are allocated to achieve qualitative and quantitative outcomes (Chapter 5). This process offers a meaningful indication of how dollars are expected to turn into outcomes, how dollars fund daily activities (i.e., the performance indicators), the required resources (Input), the expected output and the resulting outcomes.

The first step in the process is to conduct a workload analysis of the entire organization, which will help quantify effort and determine proportionate need. Reactive workload demands affect every facet of organizational capacity and may adversely influence desired outcomes. For example, if the agency is spending a great deal of time answering false burglar alarm calls, then other services may suffer such as following-up with crime victims, following-up with offenders, attending community meetings or conducting directed patrols. [19] Only after assessing the reactive workload can administrators determine how much time they will have to devote to other priorities (e.g., proactive operations and community meetings). Once the workload analysis is completed, then measures of individual (Employee) performance must be taken.

Quantifying the activities that personnel devote to each desired outcome is necessary to evaluate the effort (Input) expended to produce specific output that leads toward a desired outcome. Effort (Input) can be quantified in different ways such as the number of personnel-hours expended to perform a particular activity or to confront a problem and the number of activities performed. The starting point for effort evaluation is the baseline that serves as the initial measure against which subsequent effort (i.e., output) is measured. [20] Employee output must be quantified so individual productivity can be evaluated; this will identify under- and over-performing officers as well as measure how the organization is meeting its desired outcomes. Measuring employee output is important; however, output alone is not a measure of success. Output is the direct product of employee activities that *contributes* to program and organizational outcome; output measures provide only limited information about the impact or intended benefit of the program (See appendix 1 for an example on how to measure employee performance).

The next step is to evaluate the effectiveness of individual programs (e.g., patrol, investigations, etc.) (Chapter 2). Evaluating program effectiveness means assessing the extent to which a program has had an impact on a particular problem, whether the program's goals were achieved and how those goals contributed to the agency's desired outcome. Essentially, program evaluation gauges whether the program is a success or failure. What success looks like should be established during a strategic planning session, at the same time outcomes are identified. Asking questions such as: *What does success for the patrol division look like? The traffic division? The communications division? The investigations division?* will determine what data will be captured, what proportion of the budget must be devoted to the program, what the intermediate objectives will be and what program personnel (e.g., division commanders, middle managers, supervisors and line staff) need to do to achieve the end outcome. If employees beat the baseline measure, even though they may fall short of their intended targets (i.e., performance standards), then it is likely the program's goals will be achieved.

Lastly, overall agency performance must be evaluated, to determine if the desired outcome has been achieved. If employees are productive, if they are beating their baseline and the individual programs are performing as intended, then there is a strong likelihood the agency will achieve its stated goals. Quantifying the agency's overall performance is to determine whether there was a positive impact on the entire community; comparing baseline measures against the stated target will determine effectiveness (Figure 6). Effectiveness can be compared mathematically in relation to the resources used to get there. There are various basic and intermediate statistical techniques than can be used to analyze the data; whereas some techniques describe the data, others help to draw inferences for better planning and evaluation (Chapter 6).

Quantifying the agency's overall performance and explaining how it achieved its outcomes is commonly termed *outcome monitoring*. Questions to ask during this process include:

1) Are we doing what our mission says we are doing?
2) Are the activities still the rights ones?
3) Must we make adjustments by adding new activities and/or discarding others?
4) Are we achieving results sufficient to justify the human and financial expenditures?
5) Are the division's goals and intermediate objectives being achieved?
6) Do the services have a beneficial effect on the recipients (Citizens, victims, witnesses, complainants and offenders)?
7) Do the services have adverse side effects (i.e., unintended consequences or by-products of police operations) on the recipients?
8) Has the problem or situation the services are intended to address, been made better? [21]

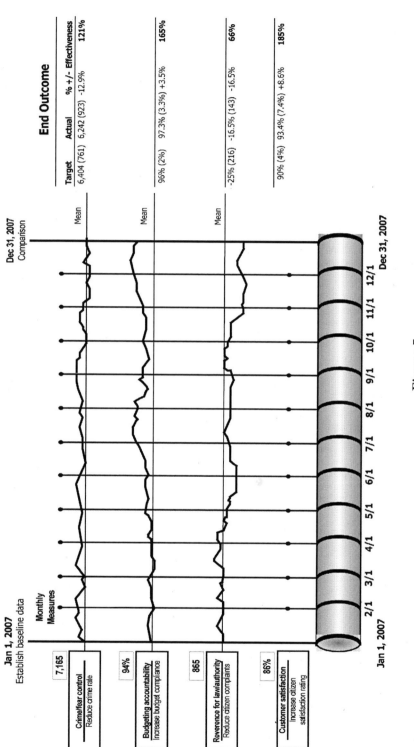

Figure 7

Figure 7 reads like this: Beginning with *Crime and Fear Control,* the baseline number of reported crimes is 7,165 on January 1, 2007. The agency sets the target number of reported crimes at 6,404 (A 10.6% reduction) for December 31, 2007 (The target is the *performance standard*). If the target is achieved, then 761 fewer crimes should be reported. As the year progresses, monthly measures of crime are taken to see how well the agency is meeting its intended outcome. During this same period, measures of individual officer performance and program performance are also assessed to see where adjustments need to be made, if any (Intermediate objectives). On December 31, 2007, the year's final measures are taken. The actual number of crimes recorded is 6,242, which is 923 fewer crimes than the baseline. This is better than expected, since the forecasted target was 6,404 crimes. Overall, crime was reduced by 12.9% from the baseline. *How effective was the agency at achieving its intended outcome?* The agency was 121% effective. The agency would have been 100% effective had it reduced crime by 761 incidents, the original target. However, the agency did better than that by reducing the number of incidents by 923, which is 162 more crimes than originally forecasted. The same logic and calculations apply for *Budgeting Accountability and Reverence for Law and Authority*. Note, the performance dimension *customer satisfaction*, does not show monthly measures. Assessing customer satisfaction is often accomplished through a community survey. Since it is not practical to survey customers each month, this example shows only the baseline data compared to a single subsequent measure (The year's end). Intervals for customer satisfaction surveys vary, but typically range between every 2 to 5 years.

The final aspect is to measure efficiency. Efficiency is the degree to which output is achieved in terms of input (Resources allocated) as expressed by ratio (Chapter 2, *Types of Performance Measures*). Efficiency is concerned with maximizing productivity (Output) while minimizing costs (Input). This is the focus of *efficiency analyses* and two typical methods are cost-benefit analysis (CBA) and cost-effectiveness analysis (CEA) (Chapter 7). The primary difference between cost-benefit analysis and cost-effectiveness analysis is whether a monetary value can be placed on the end outcome. If it is not possible to place a dollar value on the end outcome, then a cost-effectiveness analysis should be undertaken. One easy way to measure efficiency is to demonstrate a nexus between workload and costs through an activity-base budget (ABB) (Chapter 5).

An ABB is an economic model that grew out of activity-base costing (ABC), which is similar to zero-base budgeting (Maddux, 1999). An ABB is transparent and eliminates hidden costs. Not only does it afford the reader the ability to see where funds are spent, it gives a manager who has oversight the ability to see at a glance the most expensive activities and where to exercise control. This budget type accounts for the number of activities undertaken by staff members and how they allocate their effort among those activities. Once the full cost of each activity has been calculated, drivers can be established that link support activities to the primary activities of the organization-in a law enforcement environment the primary activities are the direct costs of program delivery (e.g., patrol services, investigations, tactical operations, communications, traffic control, jail operations, etc.) (Maddux, 1999). Table 5 provides an example of how chief executives and managers can exercise control by using ABB:

Table 5 Varieties of Control Exercised through Activity-base Budgeting

Fiscal Control	Management Control
Uncover waste and hidden costs	Assign personnel based upon a demonstrated need
View which activities are most and least expensive, thus subjecting them to review	Expand or contract personnel proportionately as the need changes
Assess the full efficiency of the organization	Expand or contract personnel based on how much time the organization decides to allot for service demands, administrative activities and proactive operations
Identify places to cut spending	Expand or contract span of control for management, supervision and support staff based on workload volume
Establish a cost baseline that may be influenced through process or technology changes that reduce effort requirements for the activity	Analyze the impact of nonproductive full-time equivalent (FTE) on staffing requirements (Relief factoring)
Argue from an informed, objective position in favor of the organization's budget and resource distribution	
Distribute costs for consumable supplies and depreciating equipment as part of overall per-unit costs	

Modified from Maddux, 1999:228

Linking performance to the budget, evaluating individual performance, and evaluating the efficiency and effectiveness of programs has at its core the following question: *Is anyone better off?* (Friedman, 2005:68) Answering this question is a matter of quantity (How much did the agency do?) and quality (How well did the agency do it?). The agency should be most concerned with whether there is an improved state. Rossi, Lipsey and Freeman (2004:78) offer two questions to help guide efficiency analysis:

1) *"Is the cost reasonable in relation to the benefits?"* (What am I getting for my money, as understood by taxpayers, elected officials and top police administrators?)

2) *"Would alternative approaches yield equivalent benefits at less cost?"* (Is there a less costly method that will give us *at least* the same outcomes, if not better).

These questions can serve as the premise for efficiency analysis. However, it is also important to ask different questions to determine if an *"improved state"* exists. The following questions help answer whether something *"worked,"* whether it was *"successful"* and whether the agency can express *"good performance"* for the programs it carries out:

1) What is the reaction from citizens? Are they satisfied with services? Are there fewer crime victims this year compared to last year? Are there fewer external complaints?

2) Did average property values rise over the last 2, 3 or 5 years?

3) Do the citizens "feel" safer (Or less fearful)?

4) Are outputs constant over time? Increasing? Decreasing? Why?

5) Are total costs and cost per unit increasing, decreasing, or remaining constant over time? Is the agency more or less efficient and effective?

6) How do inputs, outputs, efficiency, service quality, and outcome indicators compare?

7) What did the agency learn from the comparison process? Is the comparison information useful?

8) How did the agency compare to established targets, other organizations, or industry standards?

9) Has a "best practice" or a "better practice" been identified?

10) What can the organization change in terms of operations or organization to improve performance?

11) Are there techniques, technologies, or methodologies that other agencies are using that make them more efficient or effective than your agency? [22]

Police agencies are judged by their record of achievement. Measuring police performance is vital to achievement and has implications for personnel as well as the organization. To ensure the agency meets its desired outcomes and provides the best level of service possible, it is necessary to affix accountability across the entire spectrum of rank in the department. Accountability need not be associated with punishment, as it has so many times in the past (Friedman, 2005:87). When using a performance management framework the emphasis should be on outcomes, not necessarily compliance.

AFFIX ACCOUNTABILITY

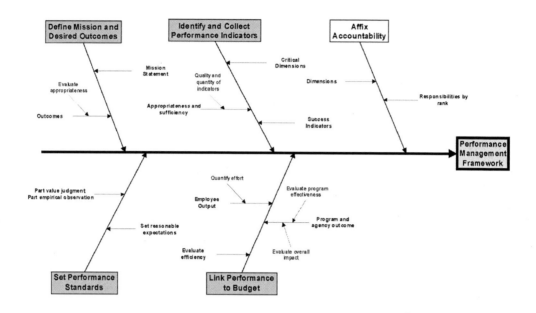

To be effective, performance management requires accountability from all levels of the agency. Public accountability means police employees have an obligation or must be willing to accept responsibility and proffer a statement or explanation of the reasons, causes, or motives to account for their actions. How much employees do (Quantity) and how well programs achieve their intended outcomes (Quality) are partly attributable to the level of accountability in the organization. Accountability requires the agency to: 1) clarify what is expected, 2) examine activities and performance measures and compare actual performance with what is expected, 3) act on findings to improve activities and performance measures, and 4) communicate findings in accordance with agency and regulatory policy; a performance management framework meets this requirement. Calling employees to account for what they do and how well they do it is a fundamental principle of management and supervision. Affixing accountability fosters responsibility on the part of managers and facilitates better decision-making by providing supervisors with information to perform their management control function.

To evaluate individual performance it is imperative to ask: *What is this rank responsible for?* After this question is answered, then the chief executive can assign responsibilities based on job description and organizational function (Chapter 2). There are four commonly recognized levels of accountability in police departments, each a subsystem of the entire department hierarchy: Administrative, command, supervisory and operational (Table 6).

Table 6 Structure of Accountability within the Rubric of Organizational Function [23]

Dimensions	Performance Measures	Accountable Rank	Level	Obligation [24]	Organizational Function
End Outcome	Controlling Fear, Crime and Disorder; Improving Citizen Satisfaction; Budgeting/Policy Compliance	Chief/Deputy Chief	Administrative	To answer for or report on what the organization *actually* accomplished, compared to what it *planned* to accomplish; accountable to the citizens and elected officials	**Overall general direction of the department:** Policy development; long-range planning; rational and comprehensive decision-making; budgeting; coordinating external requirements with organizational resources
Division Goals	Increase Clearance Rate; Reduce Citizen Complaints	Captain	Command	To share ownership of the activities and responsibilities for achieving division goals; accountable to the agency's administrative level	**Overall implementation of policies and programs developed by top administrators:** Devising strategies that capitalize on strengths, overcome weaknesses, seize opportunities and reduce threats; determining staffing requirements; devising and adjusting goal-directed strategies, as necessary
Inter-mediate Objectives	Monitor Interim Progress toward Division Goals	Lieutenant	Command		
Input Level	Train, Inspect and Guide Personnel; Apportion Allotted Resources	Sergeant	Supervisory	To provide adequate training, guidance and resources to a delegatee with a focus on the individual who must answer and report about his or her accomplishments (Or lack thereof) (Principle of unity of command)	**Overall operational control of the workforce, production of outputs and, to a degree, consumption of inputs:** Initiating actions to ensure specific activities are coordinated and carried out efficiently and effectively; devising personnel assignments; ensuring performance standards and targets are achieved
Output Level	Quantifiable Measures of Police Activity	Police Officer/ Detective/ Civilian	Operational	To look inward for initiative and personal results to improve a situation or a condition; accountable to one's self and one's immediate supervisor for accomplishments	**Overall execution of specific activities, processes and individual productivity:** Performing activities specified in policies, programs or when directed by supervisors; direct outputs that meet or exceed performance standards or targets

The final component is to report on performance. Documenting how the agency is progressing and where to make adjustments is an essential aspect of management because it keeps the workforce informed about how well (or how poorly) they are performing and where adjustments must be made in the future.

REPORT PERFORMANCE

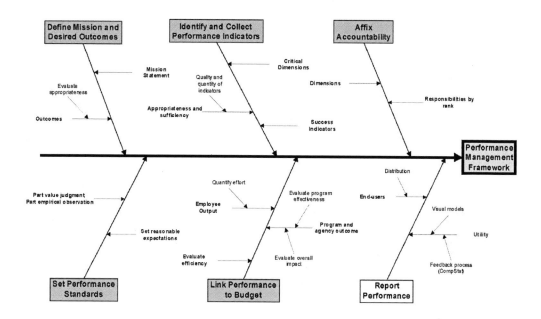

Reporting on performance is essential if top administrators are to make responsible, effective decisions and foster full transparency and accountability across the agency. Performance reports should:1) be presented in a concise easy-to-understand format; 2) be published at regularly scheduled intervals; and 3) involve all of the agency's accountable supervisors (Chapter 7, *The CompStat Process*). The utility of the reports should be such that the findings are clearly and precisely presented, especially if the document contains the results of statistical analysis. This is especially important when a command staff member, analyst or the chief executive is attempting to inform or persuade people during a lecture or a meeting or if they are trying to persuade readers of a published report, such as elected leaders or community members. It is a good idea to consult a text that specifically deals with writing about and reporting on numbers and quantitative data, if you are not familiar with the subject; one of the most widely regarded original texts on this topic is by Miller (2004). There are two ways to augment the narrative portion of a performance report that will inform or persuade people: Charts/graphs and tables (Chapter 4). Charts, graphs and tables are known as visual models and should replace narrative where possible since they use less space, yet still retain the meaning. There are several styles to choose from and each type of chart/graph conveys a different message.

Performance reports should be the focal point of a continuous improvement and feedback process, such as CompStat, which takes place regularly. Smaller jurisdictions might opt for weekly command-staff meetings instead of the CompStat process to review performance. Regardless of the approach, the feedback process is essential for directing the organization and evaluating progress toward end outcomes. The essence of organizational control is an information feedback system that enables management to respond to the information it receives. Questions that typically arise from feedback are: *Where did we do well? Why? What can we replicate? Where did we fall short? Why? What is the action plan for improvement?* This feedback process should take place with all accountable department supervisors. A separate meeting should be held to evaluate organizational progress with private and non-profit external stakeholders, if any. The purpose of a separate meeting is that CompStat or command-staff meetings typically involve sensitive law enforcement information that is not for public consumption. All end-users of performance reports should be kept informed as the reports are published. Distribution should be as follows: [25]

1) Employees should receive periodic (Weekly or bi-monthly) reports via email or during meetings. Afterwards, those reports should be archived to an Intranet so they are accessible for future use;
2) External groups should receive reports via listserv monthly;
3) At year's end, performance should be published via an annual report and uploaded to the Internet.

Reporting performance is the single best way to ensure the agency remains transparent. One of the best ways to report performance is to create a business plan that is widely distributed inside and outside the organization as well as publish interim progress reports (Chapter 2, *Creating a Business Plan.* Also, refer to the Resource CD in the primary text for sample business plans).

▶ Conclusion

LIMITATIONS

A word of caution about performance data: It has limitations! Without it, police operations would slowly stop. With over reliance on it, police operations *will* slowly stop. This is often termed *paralysis by analysis*. Performance expert Harry Hatry (1999: 5) identified three limitations of performance measurement:

1) Performance data do not, by themselves, tell why the outcomes occurred [Process monitoring does];
2) Some outcomes cannot be measured directly; and
3) The information provided by performance measurement is just part of the information managers and elected officials need to make decisions.

Performance data reveal that something occurred, or that something was achieved. However, process monitoring reveals *how* those things occurred, *how* those things were achieved. Questions to ask when monitoring process include:

1) Are administrative and operational activities being met?
2) Are the intended services being delivered to the intended persons?
3) Are there needy but unserved/underserved persons the department is not reaching?
4) Are the customers satisfied with the services?
5) Are administrative, operational and personnel functions handled well? [26]

Another important limitation is that perfect performance measures are elusive. The best researchers, scholars and statisticians recognize there is no perfect data set, there is no perfect way to measure variables of interest and interpreting and drawing conclusions involves subjectivity. Data collection is subject to human error (Jacob, 1984), which affects reliability. However, this is no excuse for avoiding performance measurement. If it were an excuse, then research and advancements in pharmaceuticals, engineering, marketing, financial investing, social or medical science would cease.

Lastly, performance data do not obviate the need for supervision especially since the model presented here does not account for intangible qualities that are important for successful policing such as judgment, leadership, emotional stability and ability to get along with others. [27] These traits must be observed and reinforced by competent supervisors and command-staff personnel. For this reason, it is imperative to treat training and KSA building as a recurring investment instead of a burden on finances and a drain on human resources.

FUTURE DIRECTIONS

The future of performance management appears certain. A new era of performance management is emerging and progressive police leaders find comfort knowing their work can be quantified, something that has not been done in the past. With hard data about what personnel are doing, a chief executive is well poised to defend the agency against criticism; they no longer have to rely on affability, impressions, conjecture or anecdotal evidence to justify their existence; and they are better able to clarify expectations, which is beneficial to employees and to the organization.

For the Employee. Performance management is encouraging for employees in terms of career incentives that match enriching assignments to performance, knowledge, skills and abilities. There are also rewards from *performance targeting*, a management practice where supervisors use performance data as a guidance, support and cooperation system instead of a punishment and rewards system (Halachmi and Holzer, 1987). In this model, supervisors can capitalize on strengths and remedy weaknesses to help employees embrace important activities before they become urgent.

For the Organization. The organization benefits from both hindsight and foresight. A learning organization [28] develops the ability to look backwards and extract useful information from data as it forges ahead. Foresight is found in imagination and proactive management. Imagination is the organization's ability to forecast future states to predict when and where crime will occur, anticipate vulnerabilities, improve resource allocation, service delivery and budgeting through scenario-based planning. Imagination also helps top administrators envision where the agency will be if they *do* and *do not* do things differently. The organization also improves its capacity by linking performance indicators to priorities. This is all part of a proactive management effort that shifts the emphasis from compliance to managing for results through continuous feedback, by pooling information for joint operations and regularly reporting on streams of data and information.

Moreover, performance measures tend to promote organizational citizenship behavior (OCB). OCB are those "job-related behaviors which are discretionary, not formally recognized by the organizational reward system, and in the aggregate, promote the effective functioning of the organization" (Moorman, Neihoff and Organ, 1993). Essentially, these are the things employees do above and beyond their job description-going the extra yard-that make for a harmonious and efficient workplace, where attitudes of commitment, trust and altruism predominate. The organization cultivates this work ethic because employees perceive the organization's decision-making systems as fair; therefore, they are more committed to organizational goals. The outgrowth of perceived fairness is workforce motivation. Kramer (1998:26) noted that, "When employees feel their hard work counts for something, they strive to do their best." Hard work brings increased productivity; the hypothesized causal sequence for increased productivity is:

Improved morale → Greater job satisfaction → Greater motivation → Increased productivity
---

Lastly, performance management helps promote organizational health. There are six attributes commonly displayed by a healthy police organization:
1) Knowing what you want to accomplish; articulating desired outcomes
2) Knowing the citizens
   a. Know what they need/want
   b. Know what they are entitled to receive
3) Knowing your core business
   a. Know the demands being placed upon the organization
   b. Know the internal strengths and weaknesses; know the external threats and opportunities
   c. Know the political, economic, social and technological (P.E.S.T analysis) forces affecting the agency [29]
   d. Why is business increasing or decreasing?
4) Adapting to the demands of the core business
   a. Monitor resource allocation
   b. Monitor officer activities
   c. Benchmark what other agencies are doing
   d. Know how to:
      i. Capitalize on organizational strengths
      ii. Overcome organizational weaknesses
      iii. Seize opportunities, and
      iv. Forestall external organizational threats
5) Knowing the employees
   a. What do employees want from their job?
   b. What motivates them?
   c. What demoralizes them?
   d. This helps drive decisions about supervision, training, recruitment, transfer/job assignment and job design
6) Regularly feeding information back to employees and constituent groups
   a. What information do employees need/want to know?
   b. What information do citizens need/want to know?
   c. How will the agency disseminate information and reach these groups? [30]

▶ Final Thoughts

Police executives have an opportunity, unlike any other period in history, to improve performance in their respective agencies. With advances in research in disciplines such as policing, public administration and business management, and the diffusion of information/technology (hardware and software, web-based applications and wireless communications), managing performance has never been easier. The implication is that new and improved methods of measuring performance, coupled with the latest technological developments, makes management less labor intensive, more accurate and more consistent. This not only helps remove barriers to implementation, but policy makers (Mayors, city managers, business administrators, city/county councils) are likely to embrace the idea more quickly because tangible results manifest in a shorter period of time.

The performance management model in this guide is a reminder that being busy *is not* the same thing as achieving results. Restated, police departments do a great deal of work every day, what do they get for their effort? Is anyone better off? It is also a reminder that there must be an institutional commitment to train and guide personnel toward results instead of relying on a rewards and punishments system (Control and compliance) that fails to foster cooperation, enthusiasm and initiative.

The general purpose of this guide is to facilitate building organizational capacity to improve service delivery. By focusing on four modes of organizational adaption that are embedded in the performance management framework, top police administrators are likely to achieve the results they are looking for with less strain and frustration:

1. *Environmental:* The agency's ability to capitalize on its internal strengths and seize external opportunities while overcoming internal weaknesses and external threats as it monitors the operating environment (the "learning organization"), instead of relying on outmoded programs and tactics;

2. *Leadership:* The agency's ability to set the overall direction for the future by identifying and cultivating emerging talented employees, so the organization's mission outlives any single executive;

3. *Management:* The agency's ability to ensure the: 1) human, financial and materiel resources are apportioned and used fairly and efficiently, and 2) authority bestowed on the police is applied consistently and judiciously; and

4. *Technical:* The agency's ability to develop core competencies in personnel, then leverage that investment with information/technology resources, so services are delivered diligently, efficiently and effectively.

In practice, a chief executive can nurture these four aspects of organizational capacity through his or her sponsorship and by becoming a process champion. Whether a performance management model by itself will explain all of the variance in organizational effectiveness is debatable, but it is certainly better than not trying at all.

▶ **Measuring Employee Performance**

Measuring employee performance is essential to organizational performance. Knowing how much employees produce (Output) is a necessary ingredient of measuring effectiveness and efficiency. The employee performance model shown here quantifies the activities police officers engage in and culminates in a score that can be ranked against a performance standard to see how well employees meet established targets. What makes this model most appealing is that it does not rely solely on the traditional activities used to measure police performance (i.e., arrests, tickets and field interrogations). Those measures are far too narrow to be informative or meaningful as a representation of the services the police provide; comparatively speaking, police officers make few arrests, issue few traffic tickets and conduct few field interrogations than they do service-related activities (e.g., attending community meetings, solving problems, resolving conflicts/disputes, tending to juvenile matters). Moreover, some states have laws prohibiting police departments from defining (Via written policy) or suggesting (Via informal practice) a specific number of arrests or tickets a police officer is to produce. [31] The better practice is to consider the number of arrests, traffic tickets, field interrogations and their ultimate disposition, as one aspect of an officer's *overall* performance. Other aspects of performance should include personnel complaints (Internal and external), attendance, punctuality, work safety, directed activities, commendations/awards, training and professional judgment, among the many.

The personnel performance report has the following sections:

1) Header
2) Performance Dimensions (i.e., desired outcomes)
3) Data Elements
4) Performance
5) Summary
6) Monthly Performance Recap Report

HEADER

The report begins with a header that contains administrative information: 1) Officer's name; 2) Precinct, if any; 3) Assigned tour of duty; 4) Total hours schedule to work for the month; 5) Total hours actually worked for the month; 6) Officer's ID number; 7) The squad assigned; 8) The month under review and 9) The year. The precinct and tour are also important because it is critical to measure employee performance against standards established for a given geographical area (Precinct) and time of day (Tour). Police officers working in other parts of the city, during different times of the day will undoubtedly experience fluctuations in workload that impact how much they can produce during working hours; a workload analysis stratified by precinct and time of day will reveal those fluctuations.

PERFORMANCE DIMENSIONS

The *performance dimensions* represent the agency's desired outcomes. They should align with the mission statement and reflect all of the things the agency wants to achieve. This model uses the four previously identified outcome measures (*Controlling Fear and Crime; Delivering Public Value through Budgeting Accountability; Reverence for Law and Authority; Satisfying Customers through Service and Accountability*). Once the agency knows what it wants to accomplish, then collecting data toward that end is the next step.

DATA ELEMENTS

The first category that is developed is the *baseline*. Baseline data should be reduced to a monthly average of a few previous years for the reporting period (e.g., if the reporting period is October 2007, then the data should be from October 2006, October 2005, October 2004 and so on). Using averages smoothes fluctuations, outliers or other anomalies in the data. The purpose of baseline data is that it serves as a reference point for officers so they know how much activity was previously produced for each performance dimension. Once baseline data is established, the officers begin generating *activity* based on the performance indicators for the particular performance dimension. The agency's first-line supervisors are responsible for ensuring the officers do what is prescribed.

Within each performance dimension lies a number of *performance indicators* believed to be valid measures of that dimension. A performance indicator is a qualitative or quantitative measurement that demonstrates meaningful steps are being taken to achieve a stated goal (i.e., the desired outcomes). For example, to control crime and fear it is necessary for police officers to generate certain activity: Effect arrests; impound abandoned cars; conduct car stops; conduct field interviews; conduct directed patrols; issue traffic summonses and conduct inspections. The metric for performance indicators is either a whole number (1, 3, 10, 25...) or a percentage, expressed as a decimal (.86 = 86%). This is because some performance indicators are measured in terms of whole units (e.g., 2 arrests; 4 traffic summonses; 8 directed patrols) and some are measured as percentages (e.g., an 86% conviction rate in traffic court; 95% of response time thresholds; 92% citizen satisfaction rating). By converting the percent to a decimal, the same mathematical functions can be used to calculate the weighting factor without sacrificing consistency.

Although data is captured on a monthly basis for the performance indicators, some indicators do not lend themselves to neat monthly measurement because the base rate is so low. As a general practice, if the performance indicator occurs infrequently or is measured on an annual basis, then using an annual measure instead of a monthly measure is preferred. For example, officers are typically granted annual sick leave that should not exceed "X" number of days. Only after an officer has consumed their allotted sick leave should the sick leave performance indicator count toward their productivity. Generally, sick leave is consumed infrequently and most agencies grant their personnel *annual* sick leave. Therefore, it is easier to keep a running sum of the few days that are consumed and only charge those days to the employee after they exceed the annual allotment. [32] The same is true for other infrequent events such as police vehicle collisions and restricted duty status.

A *weighting factor* for each performance indicator is then assigned. In constructing a composite score (Termed a *weighted score* in this model), the weighting factor is the process of assigning greater value to some performance indicators over others. The weighting factor is a numeric value that corresponds to the relative "importance" of a particular performance indicator compared to other performance indicators. Establishing the weighting factor is a value judgment, decided by the chief executive with consensus from the command staff, about how valuable that particular activity is to the agency. The weighting factor may become the source of controversy or union grievances if the weight given to individual performance indicators is (Or is perceived to be) excessive or unreasonable. For example, if arrests are weighted more heavily than directed patrols, then the union may file a grievance on the grounds that the police department is "pressuring" the officers to make more arrests because they "count for more" on the monthly evaluation. This could raise issues of hidden (Ostensible) quotas or some similar labor matter that is contrary to law. Nevertheless, some police activities are more important than others and the chief executive must decide what is best for their agency. One of the best ways to avoid an employment problem is to defer to the empirical research and demonstrated past experience about the weight a given performance indicator should be granted. This will make the weighting factor easier to defend.

The weighted score consists of performance indicators that are both added to and *subtracted* from the total performance score. Just as taking certain police action is desirable, avoiding certain action is also important. For example, conducting a directed patrol is an important activity. At the same time when an officer fails to appear in court, this is an adverse activity (e.g., the case may be dismissed for lack of prosecution). The weighted score for that performance indicator should be subtracted from the total score, since this lowers the agency's effectiveness. Similarly, if an officer uses more than their allotted sick leave or they accumulate more than a specified number of internal and external complaints, the score for those performance indicators should be subtracted from the overall score, because these are activities that should be avoided. If measuring what an officer produces is important, then measuring things the agency does not want them to produce is just as important.

By measuring the things the agency wants its employees to avoid, the agency also establishes control over certain hazards. For example, when a police officer fails to appear in court and the case is dismissed for "lack of prosecution," the supervisors in the agency should know about it. The officer's failure to appear might be a genuine mistake; the officer may not have received the subpoena; or it may be something more sinister. It may be that the officer purposely missed appearing in court to allow the defendant to go free. Perhaps someone paid the officer to "oversleep" the day of court. Failing to appear in court is a corruption hazard. By measuring court appearances, the agency can account for a case from arrest through prosecution and monitor the *outcomes* of specific cases-after all, the primary interest is in individual *results*!

Next, the weighting factor and the activity are multiplied to form the *weighted score*. The weighted score is summed for each performance dimension to arrive at a score for that particular dimension. Eventually, the weighted scores for each performance dimension are summed to create an overall performance score for all the activities undertaken during the evaluation period (In this example, October 2008). Once the weighted score is calculated, the last data component to be developed is the *target*.

A target is the part of a performance measure that establishes the desired level to be reached in a defined time period, and is usually stated as an improvement over the baseline. Targets must be reasonable given the demands placed on the agency. Like the weighting factor, targets are value judgments decided by the chief executive. The targets are set for each performance indicator, using baseline data and past experience as a reference point. They should be set to a level that officers can achieve given the other demands of their workday (e.g., community meetings, meeting with supervisors, performing administrative work). The targets are used to help calculate effectiveness, which is an aspect of performance.

PERFORMANCE

The *performance* section of the monthly personnel performance report reveals how well officers actually performed, as measured against the target and the baseline. The first element of performance is the *actual* amount of work produced. Actual productivity is the identical value of that which appears in the activity column under data elements and is merely duplicated for easy reading. What follows next is *effectiveness*. Effectiveness is the relationship of an organization's outputs to what the organization intended to accomplish and is typically expressed as a percentage. The formula is expressed as a percentage and is calculated in two parts: 1) the difference between the baseline data and the actual activity; divided by 2) the difference between the baseline data and the target data. This formula allows supervisors to gauge how successful an individual officer is meeting the established target. For example, under the performance dimension *Crime and Fear Control*, the performance indicator *Arrests for Violent Crime* shows a baseline of 2. The target is 3. The officer's actual activity is 3. This represents 100% effectiveness at achieving the stated target, (Table 7). If the officer effected 5 arrests, then they would be 300% effective (Not shown in table 7). Similarly, if the officer only effected 1 arrest, then their level of effectiveness would be -100%, since they fell short of the target (Not shown in table 7). Similarly, if the officer effected 2 arrests, then their effectiveness would appear as zero (0), because although the officer met the baseline, they fell short of the goal by one (1).

The last element of performance is expressed as a *percentage increase* (+) *or decease* (-) *over the baseline*. This measure compliments effectiveness by showing how much more (Increase) or how much less (Decrease) the officer produced in terms of the baseline; this measure does not account for the target, only the baseline. Therefore, using the same example, the officer was +50% *above* the baseline by effecting 3 arrests when the baseline called for 2 arrests. If the officer effected 5 arrests, then they would be +150% above the baseline; conversely, if the officer effected only 1 arrest, then they would be -50% *below* the baseline.

This methodology gives top administrators and supervisors a clear view of how well officers meet established targets compared to baseline measures. It also helps administrators and supervisors identify training needs, areas that need improvement and individual strengths that should be exploited. Above all, it helps administrators and supervisors monitor intermediate objectives that are critical to achieving end outcomes.

After all of the data has been captured for each performance indicator under each performance dimension, then a summary is presented with the scores.

SUMMARY

Summary Scores

The summary section consists of two parts: 1) the summary scores, and 2) the performance standard. The *summary scores* represent column totals for the baseline, the activity, the weighted score, the target score, effectiveness and percent increase/decrease over the baseline. Each of these summed for a total picture of the monthly performance. Beating the baseline score is considered "good" police performance and hopefully, this is what occurs.

Performance Standard

The *performance standard* is the column sum of the weighted score. Ideally, an officer's weighted score should be higher (Or at least equal to) than the established performance standard. If it is, all things being equal, then it is reasonable to say the officer is performing better than expected and the agency is on track to achieve its desired goals.

MONTHLY PERFORMANCE RECAP REPORT

The aforementioned structure is meaningless unless performance is compared to something. To compare the results of each officer's performance, a *monthly performance recap report* must be developed. This report shows how each officer performed compared to established standards and averages. This where individual performance is assessed; top administrators, command staff, middle managers, supervisors and employees can see how well personnel are meeting established standards.

The monthly performance recap report is merely a summary of the activities specified for the month, stratified by the tour of duty and the assignment. The header is similar, except the report is prepared by the supervisor. The next section depicts the personnel assigned to the supervisor and the scores for their activity. The total number of abandoned cars removed was eighteen; the average was 3.6. Administrators may find it useful to create average (Mean) scores to see if officers fall above or below that average. The total scores and the mean for each performance indicator are calculated to so supervisors can see at a glance how each officer performing. At the bottom of the report, the performance scores and the performance standards for each officer are transferred from the individual performance reports. The average and the standard deviation for all the performance scores is then calculated.

The standard deviation measures how far apart (How spread out) the scores are (Chapter 4). More specifically, standard deviation is a measure of the *average difference* between the scores. If the scores are all relatively similar, then the standard deviation will be low (Closer to zero). A low standard deviation means the scores are more alike (More consistent). If the scores differ greatly, then the standard variation will be high (Further from zero). A higher standard deviation means the scores are not similar and do not reflect consistency. The standard deviation is useful for examining consistency. In this example, the standard deviation is 101.758. This suggests wide variance in the performance score; the scores range from a maximum of 519 to a minimum of 272. Three officers (Doe, Smith and Jones) are above the monthly average; two officers (Anderson and West) are below the average.

One management question that stem from standard deviation is: *Why do the scores among a group of similarly situated officer vary so much?* In theory, all officers assigned to the same supervisor, working same tour, in the same geographic location should have performance scores that are relatively similar. If there is a wide difference (i.e., great variability), then it is time to pause and investigate where the variance exists. It may be as innocuous as some officers were on vacation and only worked a few days that month. Or, it may be that some officers did not meet the established targets because they were on a special assignment that took them away from the assigned duties. This is where first-line supervisor must answer for their subordinates' performance and find ways to improve it.

Monthly Performance Recap Report							
Supervisor's Name	John Bright	ID#	23564				
Precinct	Southwest	Squad	G				
Shift	1600 x 2400	Month	October				
Assignment	Patrol	Year	2008				
	Personnel					Scores	
Performance	Doe	Smith	Anderson	Jones	West	Total	Mean
Crime and Fear Control							
Abandoned Cars	3	2	4	5	4	18	3.600
Arrests							
Violent Crime	3	8	7	9	3	30	6.000
Non-Violent Crime	8	8	1	8	9	34	6.800
Warrant Initiated	8	4	4	12	2	30	6.000
Traffic Related	4	2	5	5	1	17	3.400
Car Stops	10	4	6	9	2	31	6.200
Consent Searches	3	2	2	2	1	10	2.000
Court Proceedings							
Adverse Suppression Hearings	0	0	0	0	0	0	0.000
Criminal Court Convictions	.9	0.87	0.9	0.91	0.9		89.60%
Failure to Appear	0	0	0	0	0	0	0.000
Directed Patrols	14	12	11	13	12	62	12.400
Field Interviews	29	25	21	25	29	129	25.800
Probation/Parole Home Visits	8	9	5	9	8	39	7.800
Traffic Enforcement							
Moving Summonses	32	25	33	29	22	141	28.200
Parking Summonses	40	40	24	36	25	165	33.000
Warnings	33	36	14	36	14	133	26.600
Inspections							
Alcohol	4	3	15	2	2	26	5.200
Campus Fraternity/Sorority	4	3	2	2	1	12	2.400
Firearms Dealers	5	5	0	5	9	24	4.800
Pawn Shops	1	8	1	3	5	21	4.200
Taverns	10	9	1	11	8	39	7.800
Vertical Patrols	20	11	2	9	11	53	10.600
Total						1,014	

Monthly Performance Recap Report							
Public Value through Budgeting Accountability (Annual)							
Sick Days	12	0	0	0	0	12	2.400
Restricted Duty Days	0	0	0	0	0	0	0.000
Disarmed Status	0	0	0	0	0	0	0.000
Modified Duty Status	0	0	0	0	0	0	0.000
Police Vehicle Collisions	0	0	0	0	0	0	0.000
At Fault	0	0	0	0	0	0	0.000
Contributory	0	0	0	0	0	0	0.000
Total						12	
Reverence for Law and Authority (Annual)							
Personnel Complaints							
Citizen (external)	0	0	2	0	0	2	0.400
Supervisor (internal)	0	0	2	0	0	2	0.400
Civil Lawsuits	0	0	1	0	0	1	0.200
Commendations/Awards	2	1	3	1	2	9	1.800
Prisoner Escapes	0	0	0	0	0	0	0.000
Training Hours	8	4	4	4	4	24	4.800
Total						38	
Customer Service and Accountability							
Directed Citizen Contacts	50	65	15	42	27	199	39.800
Response-time Threshold	.9	0.9	0.81	0.9	0.9		88.20%
Victim Follow-up Visits	25	25	7	25	26	108	21.600
						307	
Total Performance Score	518.90	493.76	272.89	460.43	365.70	2,112	422.336

	Personnel					Scores	
	Doe	Smith	Anderson	Jones	West	Mean	St. Dev
Performance Standard	307.8000	307.8000	307.8000	307.8000	307.8000		
Performance Score	518.90	493.76	272.89	460.43	365.70	422.34	101.758

▶ References

Alpert, G.P. and Smith, W.C. (1994). Developing police policy: An evaluation of the control principle. *American Journal of Police,* Vol. 13, No. 2.

Andrews, K. (1980). The Concept of Corporate Strategy. Chicago, IL: Irwin.

*Artley, W., Ellison, D.J. and Kennedy, B. (2001). *The Performance-Based Management Handbook, Volume 1: Establishing and Maintaining a Performance-Based Management Program.* Washington, D.C.: U.S. Department of Energy. Retrieved on January 21, 2008 from http://www.orau.gov/pbm/pbmhandbook/Volume%201.pdf.

*Behn, R.D. (2004). *Performance Leadership: 11 Better Practices That Can Ratchet Up Performance.* Managing for Performance and Results Series, IBM Center for Business of Government.

Bourne, M.,Franco, M. and Wilkes, J. (2003). Corporate performance management. *Measuring Business Excellence,* Vol. 7, No. 3.

*Brady, T.V. (1997). *Measuring What Matters: Part Two: Developing Measures of What the Police do.* Washington, D.C: National Institute of Justice. NCJ# 167255.

*Bryson, J.M.. (1995). Strategic Planning for Public and Non-Profit Organizations: A Guide to Strengthening and Sustaining Organizational Achievement. San Francisco: Jossey-Bass.

Cordner, G. (1989). Written rules and regulation: Are they necessary? *FBI Law Enforcement Bulletin,* July:17-21.

Davenport, T. (1993). Process Innovation: Reengineering Work through Information Technology. Boston: Harvard Business School Press.

Day, D.V. (2001). Leadership development: A review in context. *Leadership Quarterly,* Vol. 11, No. 4:581-613.

DeLone, G.J. (2007). Law enforcement mission statements post September 11th. *Police Quarterly,* Vol. 10, No. 2:218-235.

*Delorenzi, D.J., Shane, J.M. and Amendola, K.A. (2006). The Compstat process: Managing performance on the pathway to leadership. *The Police Chief,* Vol. 73, No. 9, September.

Drucker, P. (1990). Managing the Non-profit Organization. New York: Harper Collins.

*Friedman, M. (2005). Trying Hard is Not Good Enough: How to Produce Measurable Improvements for Customers and Communities. Vancouver, B.C., Canada: Trafford Publishing.

Gaines, L.K. and Cain, T.J. (1981). Controlling the police organization: Contingency management, program planning, implementation and evaluation. *Police Studies: An International Review of Police Development,* Vol. 16:16-26.

Governmental Accounting Standards Board. (2003). *Reporting Performance Information: Suggested Criteria for Effective Communication.* Norwalk, Ct: GASB.

Gulick, L. (1937). *Notes on the Theory of Organization.* In Gulick and Urwick, (Eds.), Papers on the Science of Administration. New York: Institute of Public Administration.

*Halachmi, A. and Holzer, M. (1987). Merit pay, performance targeting, and productivity. *Review of Public Personnel Administration,* Vol. 7, No. 2:80-91.

*Hatry, H.P. (1999). Performance Measurement: Getting Results. Washington, D.C.: Urban Institute Press.

Iannone, N.F. (1987). The Supervision of Police Personnel. 4th ed. Englewood Cliffs, NJ: Prentice Hall.

Jacob, H. (1984). Using published data: Errors and remedies. *Sage University Paper #42.* Newbury Park, Ca: Sage.

Jones, T.L. (1998). Developing performance standards. *Law and Order Magazine.* July:109 – 112. Herndon Publishing.

Indicates author recommended reading

Kalfrin, V. (February 5, 2008). Tampa's 10% crime drop: Good policing or fuzzy math? Retrieved on February 6, 2008, from http://www2.tbo.com/content/2008/feb/05/tampas-10-crime-drop-good-policing-or-fuzzy-math/.

*Kaufman, C.N. (February, 1973). The danger within: Organization stagnation. *FBI Law Enforcement Bulletin*, pp.3-28.

Kramer, M. (March 1998). Designing an individualized performance evaluation system: A value-based process. *FBI Law Enforcement Bulletin*, Vol. 67, No. 3:20–26.

LeBrec, D. (1982). Risk Management: Preventive law practice and practical risk management methods for the 1980's. Paper presented as the Annual Meeting of the National Institute of Municipal Law Officers, Miami, Fl. In G.P. Alpert and W.C. Smith (1994). Developing police policy: An evaluation of the control principle. *American Journal of Police*, Vol. 13, No. 2.

Maddux, D. (1999). <u>Budgeting for Not-for-Profit Organizations</u>. New York: John Wiley and Sons.

*Martin, S.E. and Sherman, L.W. (1986). Catching career criminals: The Washington, D.C. repeat offender project. *Police Foundation* Reports. Washington, D.C.: National Institute of Justice.

Maslow, A. H. (1943). A theory of human motivation. *Psychological Review*, Vol. 50:370–396.

Mastrofski, S. D. (March 1999). *Policing for People. Ideas in American Policing.* Washington, D.C: Police Foundation.

*Meagher, M.A. (1986). Assessing the importance of patrol officer task performance. *American Journal of Police*, Vol. 5:67-89.

Metzenbaum, S.H. (2006). *Performance Accountability: The Five Buildings Blocks and Six Essential Practices.* Managing for Performance and Results Series, IBM Center for Business of Government. Retrieved on June 14, 2006 from http://www.businessofgovernment.org/pdfs/Metzen baumReport2.pdf. p.6.

Indicates author recommended reading

Miller, J.E. (2004). The Chicago Guide to Writing about Numbers: The Effective Presentation of Quantitative Information. Chicago: University of Chicago Press.

*Moorman, R.H., Neihoff, B.P. and Organ, D.P. (1993). Treating employees fairly and organizational citizenship behavior: Sorting the effects of job satisfaction, organizational commitment and procedural justice. *Employee Responsibilities and Rights Journal*, Vol. 6, No.3:209-225.

National Center for Public Productivity. (No date). *A Brief Guide for Performance Measurement in Local Government.* Rutgers University. Accessible at http://andromeda.rutgers.edu/~ncpp/cdgp/teaching/brief-manual.html

*O'Hara, P. (2005). Why Law Enforcement Organization Fail: Mapping the Organizational Fault Lines in Policing. Durham, N.C: Carolina Academic Press.

Pace, D.F. (1989). Community Relations Concepts. Placerville, Ca: Custom Publishing.

Pateman, C. (1975). A contribution to the political theory of organizational democracy. *Administration and Society,* Vol. 7, No. 1:5-26.

Rhoades, P.W. (1991). Political obligation: Connecting police ethics and democratic values. *American Journal of Police,* Vol. 10, No. 2:1-22.

Rosenbaum, R. (2007). Just say no to D.A.R.E. *Criminology and Public Policy,* Vol. 6, No. 4:815-824.

Rossi, P.H., Lipsey, M.W, and Freeman, H.E. (2004. Evaluation: A Systematic Approach. 7th ed. Thousand Oaks, Ca: Sage.

Schroeder, D.J., Lombardo, F. and Strollo, J. (1995). Management and Supervision of Law Enforcement Personnel. Binghamton, NY: Gould Publications.

SEARCH, The National Consortium for Justice Information and Statistics. (2003). *Measuring the success of integrated justice: A practical approach.* SEARCH Special Report, Issue 2 (September). Sacramento, Ca: SEARCH.

---

* Indicates author recommended reading

Senge, P.M. (1994). <u>The Fifth Discipline: The Art and Practice of the Learning Organization</u>. rev. ed., New York: Currency Doubleday. In William A. Geller, 1997, *Suppose We Were Really Serious About Police Departments Becoming "Learning Organizations"? National Institute of Justice Journal,* December 1997:2-8.

Skolnick, J.H. (1968). <u>Justice Without Trial</u>. New York: John Wiley and Sons.

Weiss, J.A. (1996). Public management and psychology. In D. Kettl and B. Milward (Eds.), *The state of public management* (pp.118-143). Baltimore, MD: Johns Hopkins University Press.

Weiss, J.A. and Piderit, S.K. (1999). The value of mission statements in public agencies. *Journal of Public Administration Research and Theory,* Vol. 9, No. 2:193-223.

Whitaker, G., Mastrofski, S., Ostrom, E., Parks, R.B. and Percy, S.L. (July 1982). *Basic issues in police performance.* Washington, D.C: National Institute of Justice. p.xi.

Wilson, J.Q. (1968). <u>Varieties of police behavior</u>. Cambridge, Ma: Harvard University Press.---(1989). <u>Bureaucracy: What Public Agencies Do and Why They Do It</u>. New York: Basic Books.

* Indicates author recommended reading

[1] In a police department, compliance, which also connotes control, means conformity, obedience and a tendency to defer to a ranking superior, especially in a subservient manner, based on rules, policies and orders. In police organizations, obedience is characterized by submission to authority without question; questioning an order (Or rule or policy) is tantamount to disobedience, an infraction subject to disciplinary action. As the demand for, and enforcement of, compliance rises, creativity and initiative decrease, so much so that police officers adopt an *"I do nothing until I am told"* attitude, and even then, they do only as much as necessary to get by without raising their supervisor's attention. This attitude arises because police agencies are pervasively regulated quasi-military bureaucracies and it is extremely easy to violate some obscure policy or rule buried at the back of the third volume of the policy manual. Therefore, the less the officer does, the less negative attention they attract. Very quickly, many police officers do little or nothing except that which they are compelled to do, such as answer calls for service. Excessive compliance also creates hostility by setting managers and supervisors against each other and against the line officers for even the most trivial and inconsequential matters. Working under these conditions saps the energy, enthusiasm and initiative that are critical to success in a police department. By the time daily operating conditions reach this point, the agency is stagnant and is no longer considered healthy (Kaufman, 1973; see also Cordner, 1989). By placing an emphasis on results, the department is fostering support, cooperation and diligence toward articulated goals. Emphasizing results and giving employees something to strive for is part of Maslow's (1943) "hierarchy of needs theory," where employees desire the challenge of higher achievement, they want to be empowered with the autonomy to act, they want to feel affiliated and they want recognition for their efforts.

[2] Policing in the United States is extremely diverse in terms of community character (Urban, suburban, rural, mountainous, tribal), type (Municipal, county, state, special jurisdiction—public school, railroad, university, transit, bridge and tunnel, etc.) and size (Very large, large, medium, small and very small). Agency size does not affect the performance management framework presented in this guide; indeed, this framework is suitable for all types of communities and agencies. The diversity of law enforcement agencies in the United States creates different issues in terms of crime, budget, services and politics, which is precisely why a consistent management structure is important.

State and Local Law Enforcement Agencies, by Size of Agency			
	Agencies		
Agency Size	Number	Percent	Cumulative %
All sizes	17,784	100.0%	
1,000 or more	77	0.4%	100.0%
500-599	83	0.5%	99.6%
250-499	203	1.1%	99.1%
100-249	669	3.8%	98.0%
50-99	1,177	6.6%	94.2%
25-49	2,237	12.6%	87.6%
10-24	4,124	23.2%	75.0%
5-9	3,623	20.4%	51.8%
2-4	3,453	19.4%	31.4%
1	1,907	10.7%	12.0%
0	231	1.3%	1.3%
Source: Bureau of Justice Statistics, *Census of State and Local Law Enforcement Agencies, 2000*, p. 3. NCJ#194066			

[3] Following-up with offenders, particularly repeat offenders, is an effective crime control strategy. Research suggests that using tactics such as surveillance, buy/bust, record checking, residential visits and interviewing relatives and associates of active repeat offenders, when targeted, repeat offenders are more likely to: 1) be arrested; 2) have longer, more serious criminal histories; 3) be prosecuted, convicted on felony charges and incarcerated; and 4) the police officers are more likely to make arrests for "serious" offenses (Martin and Sherman, 1986:7). Anecdotal evidence suggests that following up with juvenile offenders may also help control crime (Kalfrin, 2008).

[4] Gulick (1937:13) first identified the specific content of "executive governance," then Iannone (1987:13) translated that content into the policing context. Gulick's acronym POSDCORB, which stands for *planning, organizing, staffing, directing, coordinating, reporting and budgeting,* embodies the function of those at the administrative level.

[5] A value stream in a police department is all the activities required to deliver a service, from initial request to final disposition, to the customer. The activities vary across the entire service delivery spectrum from call reception, to dispatch, to preliminary and follow-up investigation and prosecution, all of which are designed to satisfy the customer's social need.

[6] Modified from National Center for Public Productivity, no date.

[7] Artley, Ellison and Kennedy (2001:4-5) offer similar benefits to performance management, which are worth repeating here:
1. **"It provides a structured approach to focusing on strategic performance objectives.** In other words, performance-based management focuses on the achievement of results, not on the number of activities.
2. **It provides a mechanism for accurately reporting performance to upper management and stakeholders.** Performance-based management takes the guess-work out of 'How are we doing'? Because all work is planned and done in accordance with the strategic performance objectives, the end result is an accurate picture of individual, program, and organizational performance.
3. **It brings all "interested" parties into the planning and evaluation of performance.** Performance-based management brings customers, stakeholders, employees (i.e., those who do and/or are most familiar with the work), and management together to plan strategies and goals and to evaluate results. It is the antithesis of the "command and control" style of management of the past. The key word is involvement. Performance-based management involves those who should be involved in the process.
4. **It provides a mechanism for linking performance and budget expenditures.** At the beginning of the cycle, performance-based management provides a framework for showing what goals will be accomplished and what resources will be necessary to accomplish those goals. At the end of the cycle, it shows what was actually accomplished and what resources actually were used to achieve those results. Thus, performance-based management takes the uncertainty out of budget allocations and provides an effective accounting for dollars spent.
5. **It represents a "fair way" of doing business.** Performance-based management represents fairness. Decisions on budget allocations, employee promotions, work assignments, reward and award distribution, and the like are based on objective performance planning/results, not on appearance, personality, or other forms of favoritism.
6. **It provides an excellent framework for accountability.** Performance-based management ensures accountability for results. In the performance-based management framework, all actions, decisions, expenditures, and results can be easily explained, justified, and reported.

7.   **It shares responsibility for performance improvement.** In the performance-based management process, performance improvement becomes a joint responsibility between the organization and its stakeholders/customers or between the individual 7. and his/her management. This "jointness" assures input from both sides and increases involvement in the process, ownership of results, and accountability for performance."

[8] Retrieved from http://www.balancedscorecard.org/Objections/tabid/104/Default.aspx on January 21, 2008.

[9] Retrieved from http://www.balancedscorecard.org/Portals/0/PDF/BSCFinalPresentation.pdf on January 21, 2008.

[10] A S.W.O.T analysis (Strengths, weaknesses, opportunities and threats) is a critical set of steps in a planning exercise used to perform internal and external assessments. Strengths and weaknesses are internal to the organization; Opportunities and threats are external to the organization. A S.W.O.T analysis helps organizations evaluate the environmental factors and internal situations facing a project (See Bryson, 1995).

[11] Mission statements are designed to outlive individual police administrators; with the exception of catastrophic events such as the terrorist attacks of September 11, 2001 or hurricane Katrina (August, 2005), where the department's mission may change significantly, mission statements usually remain the same. What may change with a new chief executive is how the mission is accomplished in terms of different tactics or strategies. As new research in policing, public administration and business management emerges suggesting better practices, tactics and strategies should change to reflect contemporary standards. These changes overcome organization stagnation (Kaufman, 1973), which keeps the agency healthy.

[12] Goals and outcomes are used interchangeably and represent an anticipated end result that is intended or that guides planned actions.

[13] This does not mean police agencies should avoid experimenting with new or untested tactics or programs. Indeed, innovation is a key element of performance management (The "learning organization"). Specifically, this statement means that programs, which have already been evaluated for their effectiveness, that *do not* work should be avoided whenever possible.

[14] For example, the D.A.R.E program was evaluated as ineffective, yet communities across the country continue to adopt it and those who already have it continue with it in the face of evidence that it is not working as intended (See Rosenbaum, 2007; also see National Criminal Justice Reference Serv*ice Preventing Crime: What Works, What Doesn't, What's Promising*, NCJ# 171676, accessible at www.ncjrs.org).

[15] See *Alvarado v. Texas Rangers, Texas Department of Public Safety* (492 F.3d 605, July 16, 2007) (A civil suit filed under Title VII of the Civil Rights Act of 1964).

[16] Refer to Chapter 2, *Problem Specification as a Route to Better Performance*, for a framework that can help assess problems before measurements are taken.

[17] The baseline data set does not need to be ten or fifteen years of data. It should, however, encompass a good spread of the points that are being captured. This will help smooth seasonal fluctuations and anomalies in the data. As a general rule, three to five years will serve as a strong baseline; one year is acceptable; less than one year is probably unreliable.

[18] Refer to Chapter 2, table 1, for a list of more than 230 performance indicators.

[19] In September 2007, the Fontana, Ca police department adopted a "verified-response policy" to burglar alarms. After the department conducted an analysis of the amount of time they spent responding to alarms, they discovered the time was equivalent to two officer's full-time salaries. The chief determined the time could be better spent elsewhere in the department (Retrieved on October 2, 2007, from http://www.sbsun.com/opinions/ci_7008341.) Similarly, the London Metropolitan Police Department conducted a review of administrative bureaucracy and discovered the amount of time and money spent on front-line policing increased less than 1% when comparing 2006 and 2007 (Retrieved on October 10, 2007 from http://news.bbc.co.uk/2/hi/uk_news/7037365.stm).

[20] Baseline data is a data set arranged in chronological order that establishes the status of the data as of a specific date. Baseline data is used to provide a starting point for subsequent measurements and comparisons. For example, the baseline for case clearance rates may be the national clearance rate for the crime being measured, for cities of comparable size; or it may be the police department's clearance rate for last year. Baseline data is not a quota. Baseline data is empirical and derived from actual past experience, usually based on data captured over a large period such as quarterly, semi annually or annually. A quota is typically a predetermined target such as the number or proportion of arrests, summonses, field interrogations or other measurable output.

[21] Modified from Rossi, Lipsey and Freeman, 2004:78 and from Drucker, 1990.

[22] Modified from Governmental Accounting Standards Board. (2003). Reporting performance information: Suggested criteria for effective communication, Norwalk, Ct: GASB. pp.21-22.

[23] Modified from Gaines and Cain, 1981, p.17.

[24] Modified from Artley, Ellison and Kennedy, 2001.

[25] See www.lapdonline.org for the Los Angeles Police Department's "E-Policing" network–a dissemination method for bringing police information to citizens and other stakeholders.

[26] Modified from Rossi, Lipsey and Freeman, 2004, p.77-78. See also pages 171-172 for additional process monitoring questions.

[27] Examples of trait rating categories:
   1. Ability
   2. Initiative
   3. Alertness
   4. Judgment
   5. Leadership
   6. Decisiveness
   7. Job knowledge

58

8. Emotional stability
9. Personal appearance
10. Presentation of ideas
11. Suitability for promotion
12. Ability to get along with others

[28] A "learning organization" is an organization that is continually expanding its capacity to create its future (See Senge, 1994, p.vx, 14). An organization that actively monitors change in the environment, then adapts to and learns from that change typically by acquiring new KSA's (Knowledge, skills, or abilities) and applying them to improve service quality.

[29] A P.E.S.T analysis (Political, economic, social and technological) is used to identify the macro-level environmental forces affecting the agency.

1. **Political** factors include criminal and civil legislative policies (e.g., Substantive and procedural laws), employment/labor laws, law enforcement regulations, agency priorities, personnel assignments, organizational structure, community partnerships, and political capital.
2. **Economic** factors include the local tax base, external funding sources, the purchasing process, seasonality, and a discretionary budget for projects or programs.
3. **Social** factors are the cultural and demographic aspects of the workforce and the population, recruiting schemes, career attitudes, knowledge, skills and abilities, social science research and employee safety.
4. **Technological** factors include barriers to efficiency, effectiveness and individual productivity, automation, and the rate of technological diffusion.

After a S.W.O.T. analysis is conducted, the two can be combined in a matrix to monitor the conditions affecting the agency. Example:

	Internal		External	
	Strengths	Weaknesses	Opportunities	Threats
Political	Access to decision makers Mayor and city council recognition National and international professional network Experience and institutional knowledge Labor relations problem solving model	Inability to control personnel transfers and assignment Mixing line and staff functions Superfluous demands and redundant work Cumbersome bureaucracy and work schedules Frequent personnel assignment transfers	Ability to promote the agency through publications (Business plan) Partnerships with various community and academic institutions Legislative lobbying activities	Conflicting community demands/priorities Inability to control priorities Political meddling in personnel decisions

Economic	Ability to secure external funding (Grants) Competitive salary and benefits compared to private sector	Lack of equipment and supplies Lack of funding for KSA development	Grants for equipment, technology, personnel and overtime are available Tax levy on tourism to fund programs and operating expenses	Centralized, cumbersome and slow city-controlled purchasing process Inability to meet cash match on grants Cap on local property taxes Unfunded state and federal mandates
Social	Camaraderie Good reputation; cosmopolitan opinion leader Personally accommodating (Vacations and other time off) Diverse workforce Several career paths (Upward mobility)	Lack of formal education of most personnel Culture of indifference Shortage of office space Employee unwillingness or inability to assume creative risk taking Skill level of certain employees	Funding for bulletproof vests Encouraging aspiring police officers to consider the agency as their "first choice" for a police career Ability to recruit on college campuses Advances in police research (Problem solving, CPTED)	Shrinking recruiting pool Movement afoot to lower minimum hiring standards
Techno-logical	Desktop and laptop computers for all employees Blackberry© for all personnel Mobile video cameras in all cars Installing surveillance cameras citywide	Lack of updated technology; old equipment Complexity and learning curve for basic technology Lack of automation hampering efficiency	Rate of technological diffusion Advances in less-lethal weaponry Ability measure individual and agency performance via commercial software programs (No need for proprietary equipment)	Financially unable to keep pace with changing technology Cost of acquisition and implementation Some manufacturers too slow to deliver replacement parts

[30] Modified from Brady, 1997:4-5.

[31] See, for example N.J.S.A. 40A:14-181.1 and 40A:14-181.2, where a New Jersey statute prohibits police departments from establishing a "citation quota."

[32] Of course, there are exceptions. An officer could exhaust all of their sick leave in a single month and each subsequent month would be charged against them. However, it is important to remember that sick leave, for example, is usually a contractually conferred benefit and only those days that are consumed above the limit can be charged to the employee with adverse consequences.

▶ Index